November 1, 2016

Addendum to AMERICA ON THE BRINK...

Today I had the good fortune to meet a young man in his 20's at a bus stop. He was well read and very knowledgeable. In the course of our conversation, he observed that he felt a revolution was in the making and we would probably wind up with some form of a solitarian government. He did not think that Democracy was a viable form of government anymore. For me, he was a messenger from the youth and people younger than 60 in our country, who may not have a full grasp of the deterioration taking place worldwide. With this in mind, I have compiled this short list the atrocities that have taken place in the 20th Century.

Look up on the Web: 30 Worst Atrocities of the 20th Century; 10 Worst ISIS Atrocities; Joseph Stalin; Muummar Gaddafi; Libya; Pol Pot- Cambodia; Rwandan Genocide; Kim Jong-il and son Kim Jong-un;Holocaust, *Ilse Koch; The Most Evil Woman In History.* Now after viewing some or all of this: Do you Still Want A Totalitarian Government?

There is a general misconception that the violence and destruction here in America is because Democracy no longer has control. This is very true. Democracy has the most to offer and it is the HARDEST form of government to keep SAFE and STRONG. So the main questions are: HOW AND WHY. And this is the critical question to be answered through this election.

We must take a look at Donald Trump. How many of you have looked up his bio? What qualifies him to be President? Yes he is a business man and that is his sole qualification? His business practices have a very sorry record. Before you vote for him, PLEASE look up his business dealings. What college degree does have, he says: he graduated from the Wharton School studying Economics, University of Pennsylvania. There are many questions about this. What is his knowledge of Political Science? How much law does he know? What is his record on Diplomacy? How knowledgeable is he of leadership ship with people and governments? Does he have the ability to be the type President that will build consensus with world leaders who are trying to save the world from total destruction for totalitarian governments, in view of his recent criticism of some our allies and so critical of China, with who we have so many of our American companies now opening businesses their? How will he be able to have meaningful conversations with world leaders, who we are at odds with? Can he negotiate with Vladimir Putin and his designs to continue expanding the; Socialist Ideology – Communism? How much does he know of all of the above exterminations that are ongoing? How is he going to eliminate Boko Haran, and the inroads they are making in Africa? How will he deal with Russia's expansion into Syria and back the Assad regime? How will he finally eliminate IS? How will he contain Kim Jong-un, son of Kim Jong-II and his murderess rampage? What will he do IF a Third World War comes about? In other words: DOES DONALD TRUMP HAVE THE MAKINGS OF A WORLD LEADER?

PLEASE GIVE SERIOUS THOUGHT TO ALL OF THIS, BECAUSE THESE ARE THE CHALLENGES WE ARE FACING TODAY NOT JUST HERE IN AMERICA, BUT THIS ELECTION WILL HAVE CONSEQUENCES WORLD-WIDE; FREEDOM OR TOTALITARIANISM? A LARGE PERCENTAGE OF THE COUNTRY HAS ALREADY VOTED. WHAT EVER THE OUT COME ALL OF THESE ISSUES NEED TO BE RESOLVED. TIGHTEN YOUR SEATBELTS; WE ARE IN THE PROCESS OF REAPING A WHIRLWIND. ARE WE UP TO THE CHALLENGE?

In loving memory:
of my Mom

Frances Ellen Burns
March 30, 1900
To
February 20, 1998

AMERICA ON THE BRINK...

WILL DEMOCRACY BE RESTORED
OR WILL IT BE SWEPT AWAY?

PATRICIA BURNS

Judge Learned Hand: Jan. 1882 – Aug. -1961

"Liberty lives in the hearts of men and
women, when it dies, no constitution,
no law, no court, can save it."

~

"Thou shall not ration justice."

~

After a descent of a previous decision,
Judge Hand handed down the
following decision in 1950.

~

"By contrast, in the case of
United States v. Dennis,
affirmed the 1940 Smith Act
of all 11leaders of the
Communist Party of the United States
for Subversion"

ACKNOWLEDGEMENTS

And to all of the people that have posted articles and information on the internet. Your material is the source of information for this book which would have not come into existence without your contributions.

To Create Space: In the process of reviewing the book, edited the book for content. A Special Thank You.
There is not a bibliography for the book. The majority of the content is from the web or written articles as noted. I am accountable for all of the content.

Technical Notes: 1 : Since I started this book in 2013, in the process I have experienced a remarkable learning curve. I am responsible for of the presentation of this book, with the exception of a stock cover selected of setting up the book. *Living on a 'shoestring; I am a one man band'!* I did the editing myself and also the layout. The cover was selected from the stock available at the time of set up. All material, errors and mechanical mistakes are mine and I will gladly respond.

Note: 2 In this revision, I have checked some of the websites articles which have been removed; a notice was posted at these sites: "This Page Not Available," also the word, "EDIT" at the top of site. A regulation came through recently, allowing for contents to be removed without penalty.

NOTE: When going into the voting booth, ask yourself: Is Donald Trump fit to be President, keeping in mind; are your personal values helping you to make the right decision?

CONTENTS

ACKNOWLEDGEMENTS   4
FORDWORD: President John F. Kennedy's   6
                Inaugural Address
PART ONE   12
AMERICA ON THE BRINK   12
      Will Democracy Be Saved?   13
LEADERS AND LEADERSHIP   16
      Leaders   17
      The 2008 Meltdown   47
      Politics And Values   55
      Who Gets Most Valuable   63
      From Gun Control
PART TWO   72
PENSIONS, PAYROLLS, AND CUTS   74
      General Statistics   83
      Politics and Values   73
      The Value of Congressional Perks   88
      Man's Inhumanity to Man   94
      The Value of Review of Recent History
          and Possible Trends   105
      Points for Discussion-
      Updating Government   118
PART THREE
THE VALUE OF FAMILY LIFE?
      Valuable Discussions on Domestic Issues   154
      The Value of Spirit In Our Daily Lives   166
      The Value of Patriotism Is Invaluable   181

CONCLUSION   184
FINAL THOUGHTS   185

FORWARD

2016 – January 20, 1961 - In his inauguration address to the nation in 1961, President Kennedys' message how America could change the world, given by his words that gave us a clear view of what America could accomplish. I have printed the full text, as it clearly shows by contrast where we are today 55 years later.

I don't know of a more fitting time than no, to remember the Inaugural Address (55 years ago), of President John F. Kennedy, 35th President of the United States of America, January 20, 1961 (The History Place: Great Speeches Collection):

President John F. Kennedy
35th President of the
United States of America
May 29, 1917 – November 22, 1963

"...we observe today not a victory of party, but a celebration of freedom – symbolizing an end, as well as a beginning – signifying renewal, as well as change.

The world is very different now. For man holds in his mortal hands the power to abolish all forms of HUMAN POVERTY AND ALL FORMS OF HUMAN LIFE. And yet the same revolutionary beliefs for which our forebears fought are still at issue around the globe – the belief that the rights of man come not from the generosity of the state, but from the hand of God.

We dare not forget today that we are the heirs of the first revolution. Let the word go forth from this time and place, to friend and foe alike, that the torch has been passed to a new generation of Americans, born this century, tempered by war, disciplined by a hard and bitter peace, proud of our ancient heritage and unwilling to witness or permit the slow undoing of those human rights to which this Nation has always been committed, and to which we are committed today at home and around the world.

Let every nation know, whether it wishes us well or ill, that we shall pay any price, bear any burden, meet any hardship, support any friend, oppose any foe, to assure the survival and the success of liberty; this much we pledge and more.

To those old allies whose cultural and spiritual origins we share, we pledge this loyalty of faithful friends. United, there is little we cannot do in a host of cooperative ventures. Divided, there is little we can do – for we dare not meet a powerful challenge at odds and split asunder.

To those new States whom we welcme to the ranks of the free, we pledge our word that one form of colonial control shall not have passed away merely to be replaced by a far more iron tyranny. We shall not always expect to find them supporting our view. But we shall always hope to find them strongly supporting their own freedom – and to remember that, in the past, those who foolishly sought power by riding the back of the tiger end up inside.

To the peoples in the huts and villages across the globe struggling to break the bonds of mass misery, we pledge our best efforts to help them help themselves, for whatever period is required, not because the Communists (foes) may be doing it, not because we seek their votes, but because it is right. If a free society cannot help the many who are poor, it cannot save the few who are rich.

To our sister republics south of our border, we offer a special pledge – to convert our good words into good deeds in a new alliance for progress – to assist free men and free governments in casting off the chains of poverty. But this peaceful revolution of hope cannot become the prey of hostile powers. Let all our neighbors know that we shall join with them to oppose aggression or subversion anywhere in the Americas. And let every other power know that this Hemisphere intends to remain the master of its own house.

To that world assembly of sovereign states, the United Nations, our last best hope in an age where the instruments of war have far outpaced the instruments of peace, we renew our pledge of support – to prevent it from becoming merely a forum for invective – to strengthen its shield of the new and the weak, and to enlarge the area in which its writ may run.

9

To those nations who would make themselves our adversary, we offer not a pledge but a request – that both sides begin anew the quest for peace, before the dark powers of destruction unleashed by science engulf all of humanity in planned or accidental self-destruction.

We dare not tempt them with weakness. For only when our arms are sufficient beyond doubt can we be certain beyond doubt that they will never be employed.

But neither can two great and powerful groups of nations take comfort from our present course – both sides overburdened by the cost of modern weapons, both rightly alarmed by the steady spread of the deadly atom, yet both racing to alter that uncertain balance of terror that stays the hand of mankind's final war.

So let us begin anew, remembering on both sides that civility is not a sign of weakness, and sincerity is always subject to proof. Let us never negotiate out of fear. But let us never fear to negotiate.

Let both sides explore what problems unite us instead of belaboring those problems which divide us.

Let both sides, for the first time, formulate serious and precise proposals for the inspection and control of arms and bring the absolute power to destroy other nations under the absolute control of all nations.

Let both sides seek to invoke the wonders of science instead of its terrors. Together let us explore the stars, conquer the deserts, eradicate disease, tap the ocean depths, and encourage the arts and commerce.

Let both sides unite to heed in all corners of the earth the command of Isaiah – to "undo the heavy burdens...and let the oppressed go free."

And if a beachhead of cooperation may push back the jungle of suspicion, let both sides join in creating a new endeavor, not a new balance of power, but a new world of law, where the strong are just and the weak secure and the peace preserved. All this will not be finished in the first 100 days. Nor will it be finished in the first

1,000 days, or in the life of this administration, nor ever perhaps in our lifetime on this planet. But let us begin.

In your hands, my fellow citizens, more than mine, will rest the final success or failure of our course. Since this country was founded, each generation of Americans has been summoned to give testimony to its national loyalty. The graves of young Americans who answered the call to service surround the globe.

Now the trumpet summons us again – not as a call to bear arms, though arms we need – not as a call to battle, though embattled we are – but a call to bear the burden of a long twilight struggle, year in and year out, "rejoicing in hope, patient in tribulation" – a struggle against the common enemies of man: tyranny, poverty, disease, and war itself.

Can we forge against these enemies a grand and global alliance, North and South, East and West, that can assure a more fruitful life for all mankind? Will you join in that historic effort?

In the long history of the world, only a few generations have been granted the role of defending freedom in its hour of maximum danger. I do not shrink from this responsibility – I welcome it. I do not believe that any of us would exchange places with any other people or any other generation. The energy, the faith, the devotion which we bring to this endeavor will light our country and all who serve it – and the glow from that fire can truly light the world.

And so, my fellow Americans: ask not what your country can do for you – ask what you can do for your country.

My fellow citizens of the world: ask not what America will do for you, but what together we can do for the freedom of man.

Finally, whether you are citizens of America or citizens of the world ask of us here the same high standards of strength and sacrifice which we ask of you. With a good conscience our only sure reward, with history the final judge of our deeds, let us go forth to lead the land we love, asking His blessing and His help, but knowing that here on earth God's work must truly be our own." President John F. Kennedy, January 20, 1961.

2014: Then, all of the President's aspirations seemed possible. At this point in time, we are 180 degrees of where we were when this famous speech was given. The following material will show that we are at a crossroads. Have we learned history's lessons?

2016 – The picture today is dismal. 55 years later, we have become a divided nation once again, and we are at a fork in the road. Which way will the country go? A rouge element has risen and become very prominent in our political environment. The outcome could be the continued downward spiral, or will we recover the lost vision of what is best for America and *all* our people.

I have not change most of the content of this book when was written It was released in 2014 and didn't make it to the market. I have made some updates and they will be seen by this notation: **2016.**

PART ONE

AMERICA ON THE BRINK…

"Everything secret denigrates;
nothing is safe that does not bear
discussion and publicity."

John Adams - 2nd President of
The United States of America

WILL DEMOCRACY BE SAVED?

Democracy is the ultimate form of government. In my view it is also the most fragile form of government. In order to continue to be a stable governing process it requires the *majority of the public to be knowledgeable of the process and to participate through the voting booth*. This is especially true now. Remember: **NO VOTE NO VOICE**.

The following is most pertinent today. Mr. Cooke commented in this article (written 2006), that he had hoped to stimulate enough interest for people to become involved and **turn the tide of the downward spiral he saw eight years ago**. *It didn't* seem to generate enough interest then. *I hope these observations will get your attention now.*

WHY DEMOCRACIES EVOLVE INTO DICTATORSHIPS was written in August, 2006, by James Cooke – www.informationclearinghouse.info/article 14605.htm. The following are a few of the pertinent points that sum up the current conditions in our country today.

"Dictatorship has been, with few exceptions, performed in the service of a minority; *these dictatorships have always represented the interest of the financial elite....*

As corporations follow the rules of profit-making for themselves, they inadvertently create an ever-widening polarization of wealth. As the rich get richer, and the poor poorer, social conditions gradually change... Social inequality in the U.S. has had staggering increases in the last 10 years, to the point where there are now 45 million people living in poverty, 2 million in prison...

A dictatorship is thus the necessary evil born out of the natural processes of capitalism. Government is only as powerful as the corporate might behind it...

The U.S. has been compensating for its declining economic position with military adventurism to control vast oil reserves of the Middle East...

The aggressive foreign policy of the Republicans, which has found unanimous reception throughout most sections of the ruling-elite, *has created immense dissatisfaction and opposition from of the majority of the population...*

The Orwellian 'War on Terror' has proven to be the most effective strategy that both parties continue to use in order to instill fear, destroy civil liberties, and promote war... This is not some random mistake, but a deliberate attempt at intimidation for the lower half of the population, the motive for the 'war on terror'..."

Why the 'balance of power' is in the balance. Mr. Cooke goes on to say: "Behind the conservative shift of nearly every industrial country in the world is the worsening profit-crises suffered by their respective corporate managers... The process takes on an especially-dangerous character when trying to increase their positions by acquiring—by any means necessary—the world's last remaining key-resources and markets."

Further thoughts to be considered:

- If this current pattern continues this worst case scenario will be the result.

- We continue to be at war as more and more situations arise and we continue to try to stem the tide of evil that has surfaced in the Middle East. Are we in an unending war? The current Congress is in full support to continue sending aid.

- We had the 2008 financial meltdown, along with the Madoff Ponzi scheme both of which wiped out much of the middle class and billions of dollars that will never be recovered. (August, 2014, Bank of America agreed to pay back 34 million.)

- In the early 1970's President Nixon took us off the gold standard and no longer backs the U.S, dollar. In 2011 gold soared to over 1900 in the stock market. Many people rushed to sell gold items at this commanding price. Could there be later regrets?

- China is now #5 and Russia is #10 on the list of the top 10 countries who own the most gold.

- Some reports say that China and Russia are teaming up to devalue the dollar. Currently the dollar is still the benchmark for the world economy. *That is why Forbes and others predict a worldwide financial meltdown, if China and Russia are successful, or other combinations of countries attempt to do the same.*

  (No one has predicted when/if this will happen. So much worldwide money is invested in our country and ours worldwide, for China and Russia to make this happen—but again very possible. This is why Forbes and others have made projections that a disastrous worldwide financial crash will result.)

The scramble for oil deposits is in the headlines now as the process of fracking makes it possible to extract surface oil. Fracking is a process that can extract oil in the shallow layers of the earth.

With deregulation starting in the early 1980's, conglomerates are growing larger and larger (mini-empires?!) with the mergers now taking place around the world. Wealth is being concentrated into fewer and fewer corporate entities and the biggest holders will control world finances. This is having an effect on the world stocks markets. If there should be another shutdown, no country wants to be left holding the bag.

LEADERSHIP AND LEADERS

J'ACCUSE - I accuse.

"My duty is to speak;
I have no wish to be
an accomplice."

Emile Zola

No man has ever been hanged for
breaking the Spirit of the Law.

Grover Cleveland – 22nd and24th
President of the United States.

LEADERS

Webster's New World Dictionary; Third College Edition

Rightful: 1. fair and just; right, 2. having a just, lawful claim; 3. most helpful or reliable.

Leader: 1. the position of guidance, of a leader; 2. the ability to lead.

Sworn: bound, pledged, promised…as by an oath.

Duty: Conduct based on moral or legal obligation…

Rogue(ish): dishonest, unscrupulous

These types can be lethal, because they do not have the advantage of hindsight of a solid grounding in the "art of politics." They are not clever enough to know that they are in a very precarious position. One false move and they will be dropped like a hot potato. They might be hung with charges others should be taking, and they maybe be charged too.

The above definitions are simple and straightforward. But now, as much as any time in the past history of our country, we have to seriously question the leadership of people elected to Congress to be the foremost leaders to represent "We the People." Our rights, guaranteed in our Constitution, are being eroded by special interests and among them is the NRA/gun lobby as follows.

NOTE: The record shows that 35 Senators and 263 Representatives are on the pay of the NRA/gun lobby. In a televised public address, the head of the NRA, Wayne La Pierre, has very distinctly stated, "No legislation will pass the Congress on gun control." Information on this special interest's page read: *"This page is not available."* Just like the soft money question, we know that special interests have all means at their disposal to block any information they do not want to be known.

The NRA and Tea Party are joining together to change government. Membership is said to be at least four million. They are now using social media, including Facebook and Twitter.

Always looking ahead, in 2012 the **Koch brothers** sent money to all the new incoming Republican members – a total of 75 people; 63 in the House of Representatives and 12 in the Senate. **Ted Cruz (R-TX)** is orchestrating the defunding of Obamacare at the wishes of the **Koch brothers.** He is a staunch member (and one of the current faces of) the Tea Party.

NOTE: To the people who are not familiar with our Constitution, it is possible Ted Cruz (R-TX), a native of Canada, will be running for President. He has dual citizenship; he was born in Canada. His mother is Canadian and his father is a U.S. citizen.

LEADERS

At the present time we have more members in Congress that have the following behavior on blatant display.

Some leaders, who hold the highest positions in Congress, have been in the glaring spotlight of TV news for quite some time. They are obstructionists in the purest sense of the word. Their repeated stance of opposition to the President and has been ingrained in our minds from the first day of the then newly elected President's first term starting in January 2009.

'The High Art of Politics' has been pursued for millennia. The opposite side of this coin is *'The High Art of Manipulation.'* The following people have taken the high art of manipulation into dizzying new heights.

The ones I am pointing out does not touch the surface of what is unseen. These people are merely clues as to what is really going on and how far they have gone. From what is appearing on the surface, the phrase "Houston, we've got a problem" – (Texas) could never be more true than it is today! A state that is full of sidewinders, rattlers, vipers, also scorpions and many other very poisonous critters (people).

A must read book written by a Republican: *The Politic of the Rich and Poor, Kevin Phillips, Harper's 1991.* On the title page **USA Today** wrote, "Incisive…A devastating critique (of the Reagan Administration) that has already fueled furious pros and cons in

Washington. Kevin Phillips is Republican. This may have added to the furor at the time the book was released.

(It is my hope that you will keep this book handy and refer to this information to "refresh your memory" for upcoming elections. It may also serve as another reminder in the national elections in 2016.)

The following quote defines a climate in the political world and *should be* a reference in the world today. The following quote from the Polish poet:

Czeslaw Miloz: Nobel Prize in Literature

"In a room where people maintain a conspiracy of silence, one word of truth sounds like a pistol shot." –

Czeslaw Milosz, 1911-2004 – By Leon Wieseltier, Sept. 12, 2004.

"The death of a man is like the fall of a mighty nation." Declared Czeslaw Milosz in one of the many poems in which he speculated upon the experience of dying. The poem explains that the fall occurs because the nation is no longer mighty, its population is dispersed..."its mission forgotten its language is lost." Yet it is the death of this man that is like the fall of a mighty nation, but a nation full and undispersed, its mission honored and its language imperishable..." from the beautiful eulogy to this Nobel Prize in Literature winner.

NOTE: The following information is provided by **sourcewatch.org** and **dailykos.com.** Please go to these websites and read their full reports. These websites have very generously given permission to use their material. Mr. Miloz wrote extensively about communism and the turbulence after World War II.

By now I know that everyone is clear that in my view, very serious changes need to be made. These issues need to be brought to the forefront. We cannot wait for the right time to start to do something. We have to start now to find the most qualified people to run for office in the 2014 election. We have to replace those that are known to be obstructive that are still in office. In my view they should be prosecuted for failing to perform their duties as sworn when they took the Oath of Office.

Added to the above, are the **KOCH** brothers, who backed the founding of the **American Legal Exchange Council (ALEC)** in **1973.** This group started the process to legally change our laws and judicial systems. **(See page 30 for detailed information about the Kochs.)**

The stock market and the banking world, reshapes itself too. At the top are the people in the money world--the power brokers. The decisions they make determine how the flow of money progresses in the daily lives throughout the world and it is always ahead of the curve they create. It operates on its own time and pulse.

If enough people in these top circles can make more money by creating havoc, through protracted warfare and any form of destruction, that is the direction the flow of money will go. At this time it is apparent this is the pattern we are in and why some people are predicting that we are headed for the ultimate showdown.

George Santanya: *"If you don't know past history, you are bound to repeat its mistakes."* I add: *"*You are known by the company you keep."

~

Generation after generation will continue to reveal 'hidden messages' until all of the truth is out. How the Presidents' George H. W. Bush and George W. Bush became so entwined with these rouges is to be left to history. But it was on the watch of President George W. Bush, that our country was brought to its knees resulting In the 2008 meltdown.

~

CURRENT CONGRESSIONAL RATINGS

APPROVAL RATINGS – **Most polls show these figures. The could vary 1-3%**

10/2013 Republicans **26%** Democrats **34%**

8/2016 – Just 20% of Republicans think their elected Representatives are doing a good job. By contrast, Democrats 64%.

Over all, REPUBLICANS 16% Democrats 17%.

Harry Reid **43%**, Mitch McConnell **35%**, Nancy Pelosi **31%,** and John Boehner **20%** (including his home state of Ohio). **2016 - *John Boehner step down 9/2015, and *Paul Ryan new speaker 10/2015. Note: no new ratings at this time.**

(Polls vary because of the time they were taken after a bill has passed or failed. There are many sites to check for specific information.)

*A report by the Washington Post **10/13/2013 on the worst Congress** shows the current Congress at the bottom with only **72 bills passed** by the end of last year and only 15 have passed this year. Most recently one poll showed that **87%** disapprove of this Congress and feel that our system is broken*www.slate.com **TO DATE THIS YEAR** – Only 15 bills have passed with over 4,000 submitted. Most of the bills that passed were of relative importance to individuals. The one significant bill S716 …modifies the requirements under the **STOCK Act** regarding online access to certain financial disclosure statements and related forms. **A disemboweling of the ban on insider trading by Hill staffers.** *(The bold is mine, the sentiment is that of the writer. **NOW** this is another deregulation for the benefit of the financial world.)*

Senator Harry Reid (D-NV): First elected to the Senate in 1986 and has been Speaker since 2007. Always considered a moderate and a consensus builder his ratings have dropped with a deep slide in the current climate in Congress.

Congresswoman Nancy Pelosi (D-CA): Was first elected to the House in 1987. She was Speaker from 2006 to 2010. She was not effective in countering the Tea Party and her deep slide also shows.

Senator Mitch McConnell (R-VA): Was first elected to the Senate in 1986. No doubt that he is a master of disguise. His policy of favoring the narrow right has never changed. It is surprising that his rating is still so high. **2016 - More**

Congressman John Boehner (R-OH) – Speaker of the House. 2016 – He stepped down on September 25, 2015 because of pressure he was under for not following the party line. He was very conservative to begin with. The more militant ruled.

2016 – A side note: I find this to be very interesting. When John Boehner let office, after being in office for 25 years (1990 - 20150his net worth was: **$2 million**, Paul Ryan has been in the house 15 years and his net worth today is **$7.3 million.**

2016 – THE ROGUES: FOCUS ON SOME OTHER KEY PLAYERS.

Donald Trump – As noted above.

Paul Ryan – Speaker of the House and 3rd in line for the Presidency: I have written much more about Paul Ryan to follow. Another illustration that has taken place in this campaign is the following scenario that played out on Facebook. Will he, won't he... run for office? Finally no he would bow to Donald Trump with reservations. Again: Will he, won't he, yes he will but... Then it was Trump's turn: Will he, won't he... endorse Paul Ryan... and then yes after much encouragement from the "party supporting him", he will endorse Paul Ryan.

Now they have both gotten their heads together, as to eliminate Social Security and follow through on the long lists of the sweep of our Democracy as we know it today. It is my belief that Paul Ryan in his time in Congress, a very early advocate of the Kochs and not as a fan of Ayn Rand as he demurs. **See (page 27)**

DIS-INFORMATION (placing false information): this is the lead story today and of a rightful concern for our government and intelligence agencies. This tool has been widely used throughout the world in the game of politics ands for a very long time and right up to today. "The Russian government hack of the Democratic National Committee disclosed by the DNC in June, *but not officially ascribed by the U,S, government to Russia…* further: …**Senator Ben Sasse (R) of Nebraska** "in a public statement urged Obama to publicly name Russia as responsible for the DNC hack… This kind of comment coming from Senator Sasse, just adds inflammatory rhetoric to an already heated environment for this issue and this election. Also **FOX News** through Dis-information is the standard for their distribution of this type news information.

2016 -http://www,wikipedia,org/wiki/Roger **Criticism of Roger Ailes** In January 2011, 400 Jewish Rabbis call Rupert Murdoch, Chair of News Corporation to sanction Glen Beck for his use of the Holocaust to "discredit any individual you disagree with" when putting down the Holocaust. Ailes commented: "the left rabbis" and called **N.P.R.** News, later apologized for the remark, but not to **N.P.R.**

Roger Ailes – Encouraged by Rupert Murdock, Roger Ailes founder Fox News in 1996. Jeff Gillenkerk wrote the fiction novel **Dark Pursuit** of which N.P.R.'s Margot Ader commented " A gripping page turner… the best of the lot. There are games beyond games; real insights into the political machinations of Washington and the clueless nature of even the best media." The book was written to expose what Mr. Gillenkerk had learned re: Roger Ailes. Ailes has had to step down recently, because of his "sexual harassment suit." Rupert was asked to take the helm.

Fox News has been the voice of the ultra-right since 1996 and has advised the Republican Presidents. He was notably behind President Regan's time in office, at Regan's request. Regan held Ailes in high esteem.

The Republican Senate Minority Leader Mitch McConnell

The first person to be reviewed is Mitch McConnell. He was first elected to the Senate in 1986. Mitch McConnell has been the Senate Minority Leader since 2007. From the time of the first term of the current President, he vowed to make every effort to see that this President would not serve a second term. History showed otherwise as the President is now in his second term. The President even won in the home state of the Senate Minority Leader. One has to wonder about the popularity of this Senator if the opposition party President won in his home state.

2016 - This summer he vowed that he will not confirm the vacant seat on the Supreme Court, until President Obama is out of office

March 23, 2013 – *The latest information on this Senator: He voted to prohibit the United States from entering into a United Nations Arms Treaty.*

Note: What follows is from the below websites. It is because of the altruism of websites such as these that we are able to bring you pertinent information that is important for the general public to know, not just people who have a particularly strong bent for politics.

http://dailykos.com/story/2010/12/05/925858/

http//:dailykos.com/story/2010/12/05/925858/

How Senator Mitch McConnell became very rich by devtob. Dec. 05, 2010

It seems, from review of his financial disclosure forms, that the Senate Minority Leader's wealth has jumped substantially in the last few years. Back in 2005, his net worth was somewhere between $1,645,032 and $4,278,899, ranking him the 38th richest Senator.

After four years when the stock market had flat-lined, the Senator's net worth was between $7,102,036 and $32,756,000 and he is now the 12th richest Senator, (the height of the wars). This is pretty good for a guy who has evidently never had a private sector job.

Obviously, the wide range of the Senator's wealth is due to the way the disclosure forms allow a pretty wide range on reports of assets. His top assets are his holdings in the Vanguard Tax Exempt Money Market, estimated to be between $5,001,002 and $25,015,000. The rest are investments in a wide variety of stocks and bonds mutual funds.

Let's look at his Vanguard investments. Back In 2006, his major Vanguard investment was in its 500 Index Fund, estimated at between $650,003 and $1,350,000. The next year, his wealth in that fund jumped to an estimated $1,100,002 to $5,250,000 ($4,150,000.00 more) Then in 2008, *not a good year in the market*, his wealth in the fund dropped a bit (estimated from $500K to $1M), but all of a sudden he had, $5,001,002 to $25,015,000, in the Vanguard Tax Exempt Money Market.

The year before, he had a pittance ($1K to $15K) in that fund. Somehow, someway, he got much richer in 2008. It appears that somebody could be his second wife's father, who made a fortune in shipping Chinese-made goods to the USA.

Senator McConnell and his second wife Elaine Chao were married in 1993. She was the President Bush's a*nti-Labor Secretary of Labor* for a full eight years.

According to Laura Flanders, her father, James Chao, had the luck to attend one of his country's finest universities with Jiang Zemin, the future leader of the People's Republic of China, who fell in with the immensely powerful Shanghai-born family the Tung's, who shifted their operations to Taiwan for a time.

The Tung dynasty is powerful in Chinese politics to this day. Hong Kong's first chief after reunification with mainland China was Tung Chee Hwa, the first child of the magnate Tung Chao Yung, in whose Maritime Trust company James Chao got his start. James Chao married into another powerful family: the Hsus. His wife's family would later operate a shipping empire in Hong Kong.

So, Senator McConnell has moved from the upper-middle class of a lifelong government employee into the upper class ($20M or so net worth) of someone who married a wife with a rich father. Who just happened to become rich from his connections with the current rulers of Communist, China.

Villagers would say that this is old news; "free" trade is great for everybody. We like (this couple), and we want them to return our calls, etc."

So they have not reported the source of Senator McConnell's mega-wealth (relative to the rest of us), and how that source has presumably, for 20 years or so, affected his position on "free" trade and its devastating impact on millions of Americans who used to have decent manufacturing jobs.

Senator McConnell and his wife are cheap labor Republicans who hate the idea of American factory workers making more than $15 an hour.

Because that's what their benefactors want them to do.

www.prosense.com – Joan Carter – June 19, 2012

Reinforcing the above position, Senator McConnell said *"The poor have it too easy; they have to pay their share of taxes…"*

Also thinks our tax system is "too damn progressive…and the tax code should be restructured to make it fairer to upper income earners."

NOTE: This is the latest action by Senator McConnell*** to tie the hands of the United States of America. He is also planning to filibuster the hearings on gun control, which are now being held. June 3, 2013, the Senator's latest effort to curtail more of the Freedom of Information Act* *also wants to limit information on who donates money to a candidate.* Seemingly, he has complete disregard for the laws of the land. If this position were to take effect, it would be a further erosion of our Democratic form of government. ***See Citizens United Supreme Court Case: pg. 34.**

Senator McConnell's position on the following issues is strongly in favor of rights of big business and interests. These positions reflect

his positions since the year 2000.

- **He is a "war hawk"** – has supported the Iraq war; against troop pullout.
- Against 9/11 terrorist prevention. Against Disclosure Act for openness in government.
- Said: "Without Soft Money Republican Party would not exist."
- Questionable position re: marked funds for British contractor.
- Although Kentucky is a red state, "voters are exhausted by his obstructionist tactics."

A fellow Senator is to have said, "The only way he can win the next election (November 2014) is by a dirty campaign." Senator McConnell has been likened to the late President Richard M. Nixon and his obstructionist rule during his terms in office.

NOTE: His positions on labor, outsourcing jobs, trade limitations, pro-gun lobby/NRA, and a stance on many other issues has contributed to a weakening of America's position in commerce and trade, of gun sales and protection of gun manufacturers throughout the world.

www.sourcewatch.org/index This Source Watch report is 11 pages long. Some of the controversy that was in this report includes his position for:

- Is anti-labor and was a strong proponent of outsourcing trade to China.
- **"Pushes Bill to Block Obesity"** lawsuits of junk food seller. Rakes in money from Food, Beverage and Tobacco interests – 2003.
- **John Aravosis** "GOP Senator Flip-flops on amnesty for Iraqis who kill US troops. Republicans are divided as this issue grows."
- **CNN.com: Senate GOP leader says he'll fight Iraq pullout bill.**
- Citizens for ethics.org: (listed in) the 22 Most Corrupt Members of Congress, September 18, 2007.

*** Senator McConnell refused to give answers to a *Political Courage Test* when asked by the leaders of both parties, the media and by the project Vote Smart President, Richard Kimbal and the project staff.

2016 - While Senator McConnell overcame the above by continuing to be elected to office, *it does raise the question of his lack of willingness for compromise.* Certainly his attitude for his years in Congress, leaves one to question his ability to work for his constituency and casts a long shadow over his sincerity, when he took the Oath of Office and of his leadership as the highest ranked of the Republican Party. I read further about his wife, Elaine Chao, before they were married in 1993

With his wife's relatives in the highest offices in Communist China, does this raise any questions about their commitment to our Democratic form of government? I raise this question, because of obvious disregard for the working man and promoting the cheapest labor possible, with no benefits.

www.infoplease.com/spot/bushcabinet

Elaine Chao who was Secretary of Labor for the full eight years in President G. W. Bush's Cabinet .The selection of the Bush Cabinet members, give interesting information, through some to the bios of the members. To follow up for further information, please go to this site It was in reading through this site, that I learned that, Dick Cheney was President Gerald Ford's Chief of Staff. He was brought into this position when Donald Rumsfeld became Secretary of Defense.

www.notablebiographies.com -   In space bar enter the name of who is being researched. Elaine Chao's biography starts in China where her parents were residing, before moving to Taiwan. Her father James SC Chao immigrated to the United States first. After his business was successful the whole family moved here. He is founder of Foremost Maritime Corp. which became a lucrative business by shipping between the U. S. and China.

Elaine Chao and her father had extended ties to China's President Jiang Zemin, from they attended college together and the friendship continued was. A person who had knowledge of the family said: their contact was regular and deep.

Prior to becoming Secretary of Labor in the Bush Administration in 2001, among other positions that she held, she joined the Heritage Foundation, found by Joseph Coors, son of Adolph Kohrs, who changed the spelling to Coors after he came to America, when he founded the Coors Brewing Company. (see Wikipedia.com/coors0 for details and the connection of the Kochs funding of the Heritage Foundation.

~

"The power of the purse may, in fact be regarded as the most complete and effective weapon…for obtaining redress of every grievance." James Madison

~

"Timid men prefer the calm of despotism to the tempestuous sea of Liberty."

Thomas Jefferson
3rd President of the United States

~

Congressman Paul Ryan - Budget Chairman

Budget Committee Chairman Paul Ryan, a Tea Party favorite, who was just defeated in his attempt to become the Vice President, is back in his seat as Chairman of the Budget Committee. While in college, he worked at odd jobs before running for Congress, some work in finance, as he worked in a variety of jobs after completing college with a double degree in Political Science and Finance. The majority of his financial experience is from working in this committee.

His record shows that he has limited public sector experience. Nothing has been noted of any experience in the private sector working with corporate budgets and most notably *no experience in*

30

budgeting for systems such as DSHS or in the whole field of public aid for the needs of the general population.

Another mole of the **Koch brothers,** he was elected to his first seat in Congress at the age of 28. His narrow experience shows that he does not have a broad enough background to be on this committee, let alone his lofty position as Chairman. No wonder he is a prime candidate for the position of Budget Chairman, who by the way, is there by the Speaker's choice.

He is the favorite of the Republican Party because his policies are *a must* for this party to enhance their wealth (at the expense of the majority of Americans). He is 'hand in glove' with Capitalistic Big Business. He has attended secret meetings with the **Koch brothers,** and it is not known how long he has been associated with them. It has been said that he was an early admirer of Any Rand, but he demurs.

http://.www.billymoyers.com/2013/08/22paul-ryan-choice-constitutents-or-koch-brothers - **John Nichols***
When the City of Kenosha, Wisconsin, was preparing to *formally petition Congress to take the necessary actions to* get corporate money out of politics and to restore grassroots democracy, their Congressman Paul Ryan was secretly meeting with the **Koch brothers** to plot election strategies and policy agendas…

Sixteen states and roughly 500 communities have petitioned Congress to support a CONSTITUIONAL ADMENDMENT to restore the power to the people…by placing limits on the influence of big money, especially corporate money, in American politics.

The official calls from states across the country…*come in response to the high court's decision to remove restrictions on corporate spending to buy elections which capped a series of rulings that undermined limits on the power of wealthy Americans to dominate the political and governing process of the nation, with unprecedented infusions of campaign money.*

***John Nichols, a Washington correspondent for 'The Nation'** and associate editor of The Capital Times in Madison, Wisconsin.

He has written several books, the latest *The "S" Word: A Short History of an American Tradition.* He is also co-foundering of the media reform organization Free Press.

NOTE: I hope the above information will encourage immediate, strong debate for the merits of a Constitutional Amendment for: **Term Limits for Congress.** I suggest three terms for the Senate and Six terms for the House of Representatives. Since the population in America has doubled since World War II, we need to have a change of voices to reflect the views of our wide makeup of our citizens from every country in the world. This would be approximate 20 years+/minus for the Congress. It would also help to prevent an embedded core to take over again.

I also feel it is time to look at the Supreme Court. This would also require a Constitutional Amendment. Again citing the above reasons, I think that age 70 would be a sufficient time of service on the Court. Younger appointees are now in line with a younger population. Very much debate on both of these proposals hopefully will start after this current election.

I would also include the need to have revised rules for the Budget Committee. A realistic budget should cover the whole enterprise (in this case running our National government and the lives of all Americans) and cuts that need to be made should be spread through all entities.

Because the House Budget Committee funds the workings of our government, this Chairmanship needs to have a person who has a background of knowledge and some experience working with large budgets outside of Congress. This Chairman is sadly lacking. The Budget Chairman's view of how he sees his role I find questionable. *He proposed for the 2012 budget to cut $5.3 trillion in ten years... "We have a debt-driven crisis. And so we have not just a legal but a moral obligation—to do something about it."*

Additionally, Ryan voted against the comprehensive deficit reduction plan drafted by the bipartisan Simpson-Bowles commission, *a report which he later criticized the President for not adopting what he, voted against.*

On immigration…he called for reform (but) has stated that "any immigration reform should not allow for amnesty for the workers that have been in the US illegally for many years, *even if those workers pay taxes and are law-abiding."*

SEEDS OF DISTRUCTION - THE KOCH BROTHERS

www.salon.com/2016/01/12/Koch-father...
Fred Koch, according to the book "Dark Money" by staff writer Jane Mayer for The New Yorker, "Koch helped build the third largest oil refinery, in Nazi Germany in the 1930's. The project was approved personally by Adolph Hitler. The oil refinery fueled German planes, helping the Nazis carry a campaign of genocide and destruction across Europe."

The Koch empire "have quietly assembled, piece by piece, a privatized political and policy advocacy like no other American in history, that today includes hundreds of donors and employs 1,200 **full-time staffers in 107 offices around the world."** "That's about three and-a–half times as many as the Republican National Committee and its arms, had on their payrolls last month" Political reported.

"And the staggering sum the networks plans to spend in the 2016 run up cycle—889 million—is more than double what the RNC spent in the previous presidential cycle."

(2016)www.rolingstone.com/political/news/inside-the-koch
This expose, released in 2014, is a must read. This Rolling Stone paper is the most extensive coverage of the Koch Empire. Because of copyright laws, with a few words, I have extrapolated some of the key points. These points are only the very slightest tip of the content.

INSIDE THE KOCH TOXIC EMPIRE

The opening paragraph: The enormity of the Koch fortune is no mystery. The Koch's are our home grown oligarchs; the cornered the Republican politics and are attempting to buy Congress and the White House... Koch touts only one topline financial figure of $115 billion in annual revenues, as estimated by Forbes... larger than, IBM, Honda, or Hewlett-Packard. The Companies stock response to reporters: "We are a privately held and don't discuss this information... not entirely opaque under Charles Koch near five decade reign... top three polluters out of 30, Koch Industries comes in third.

In 1929, Universal sued (then) Winkler-Koch, accuse of stealing its intellectual property... with his domestic property tied up in court, Fred (father) started looking for partners abroad...started doing business with the Soviet Union where Joseph Stalin had just his first five year plan... building 15 cracking units... went to the USSR and "found a land of hungry, misery and terror...but agreed to give the Soviets knowledge so they could keep building more... in 1934 went to work in Hitler's regime, building the third largest oil...to fuel planes and war equipment... resulting in the 600,000 death camp atrocities and total devastation of Europe.

Later Koch... implored "Do not cooperate voluntarily, instead resist whenever and to what you can in the name of justice."... there's big money in dirty oil (money their only goal)...embargo hit hard...made a deal with Qatar exports... up to a half billion dollars... resulting in over charging American customers. In 1974, the Ford Administration... compelled Koch to pay out more than $20 million in rebates and future price reduction... more infractions, 1980, Koch Industries pleaded guilty to five felonies, Federal Court including to commit fraud...more charges of "stealing"...$31million in Native oil.

1980 David Koch runs for the Vice Presidency running on the Libertarian ticket... soured on Libertarians... dedicated to Bob Doyle of Kansas... business practices result in special Committee to be called...who ran interference... in committee hearing: "don't rush to judgment... citing concerns about some of the evidence... went to Grand Jury then dropped... Koch avoided the criminal case but... received punishment under False Claims Act which allow a private to sue government...   bill sued the company of ...defrauding the Federal Government of royalty income... on purchase of native oil... testimony submitted more than 24,000 false claims, exposing Koch to false claims... resulting penalties of $214,000 million in penalties. Koch later settled, paying $25,000 million.

During the Clinton Administration... BTU tax came up. Koch Industries could not compete... over time, may have destroyed our business... established Citizens For A Sound Economy... grass roots efforts... David Koch called it... "a sales force" to further political gains...bragged CSE's campaign played a key roll in defeating the Administrations, plans for a huge and cumbersome BTU tax... an ever growing downward spiral of machinations re: their lack of repair of pipelines... and ever endeavor to stop the downhill slide... by this time the case had come to trial, however George W. Bush was in office and the indictment had been significantly pared down... Koch faced charges of **only seven counts,** the Attorney General, John Ashcroft plea bargained... settled a "sweetheart deal" and Koch pleaded guilty to **only a single count**... no criminal prosecution...and paid $20 million in fines... and reparations—another Historical Judgment.

EPA was about to bite... in the form of record civil and criminal financial penalties... Story moves to Lively, TX. On August 24, 1996, at 3:34 pm. in the mobile home of Daniel Smally. His daughter Danielle Smally was to leave for college, she and her friend Jason Stone was there. Danielle began to feel nauseated **"Dad I smell gas"**...

The Smallys were too poor to own a phone, the teen jumped into her Dad's 1964 Chevy pickup truck to alert the authorities... the driveway crossed a dry creek bed. Danielle cranked the ignition and a fireball engulfed the truck... "You see two children burned o death in front of you—never forget that," Danille's father would later tell reporters. A line of liquid butane—literally lighter fluid ran through the subdivision.

The National Transportation Board cited "the failure of pipeline from corrosion...on inspection... found 538 defects... industry term like Swiss cheese...pipeline was gone... but 88 were repairs were made...enough to pass more testing... "Let Koch take their children out there and put them on that pipeline, open it up and watch them die, Danny told the jury and then tell me what it's worth. The Jury awarded Smally $296million-the largest wrongful death award in American history.

In his 2007 book "The Science Of Success" Koch begrudgingly acknowledged his company's is reckless; while business was becoming increasingly regulated—we keep thinking and acting as if we lived in a pure market economy. The reality is far different.

Then G. W. Bush entered the White House in 2001, his campaign fattened with Koch money... "cronyism is nothing more than welfare for the rich and powerful. Koch and Bush generated nearly 20,000 pages of records a according to a FOIA request of the G. W. Bush Library. (NOTE): There is no record of a Koch pardon in this administration time in office, either.

And the saga goes on and on... a... "I'm going to ride my bicycle till I fall off" said Koch, now 80 years old. **Question: Do you think he will fall off.?**

2016 – Charles Koch said that their meetings were no longer secret, and they will continue to have their annual meetings.

www.open.salon.com/2012/02/how-citizens-united-kept-the Koch Brothers Out of Jail   Dr. Stuart Jeanne Branhall
The Koch Brother's Long History of Flounting the Law Koch Brothers Reprieve: "further environmental violations over malfunctioning oil equipment, (the Koch Brothers) faced charges, that if convicted could be fined up to $352 million, plus possible jail time for all other executives that were also involved."

Citizens United -- A PAC was founded in 1988 by Floyd Brown, a longtime political consultant, with the **Koch** brothers who own the second largest privately owned company in the United States.

NOTE: In April, of this year the Supreme Court decision in the Citizen United case voted 5-4 to lift further restrictions on donations to political parties.

The **Citizens United** case heard by the Supreme Court in 2009 ruled in favor of big money interests "in a 5-4 ruling, the Justices declared unconstitutional the government restriction on independent political spending" As a result, the decision has paved the way for unlimited spending on elections.

www.alecexposed.org/wiki/What_is ALEC%3F
Currently, although vehemently denied by The Tea Party, Koch money is behind that group, and is heavily invested in other efforts to gain full control with the neo-conservatives; there has been a connection with the Koch brothers and Cheney through a group known as **ALEC FAQ**.

From the above website: This group is not a lobby. **It is much more powerful than that. It has become a third party under the guise as a non-profit.**

Through **ALEC**, behind closed doors, corporations and state legislatures the changes to the law they desire that directly benefit their bottom line...They have their own governing board... they work through state legislatures...ALEC boasts that it has over 1,000 of their bills introduced by legislative members (Republicans-one Democrat) every year, **with one in five of them enacted into law.**

ALEC's operating model raises *many ethical and legal concerns.* Each state has a different set of ethics laws or rules. (These need to be brought in line across all states/mine), Wisconsin...requires legislators who go to events...pay on their own dime, yet in many states, legislators use public funds to attend ALEC meetings,

37

according to one study. The long-term representation of Koch Industries has had influence over an untold number of **ALEC bills.**

Note to Readers: Looking up who has connections with this group will get you started on the path; it's easy to follow, once you get a tag. **Make no mistake, laws that have been formulated by this group since 1973 are on your books in your state and every state in the union; that's a lot of years and people to cover.**

Money is neither good or bad it is just a medium of exchange. It is how it is used--to promote the positive/good technology, science, medicine, electronic age; or the negative (bad) wars, people tearing down governments. Since the beginning of time, money has regulated all aspects of life as we know it.

Like any industry, the banking world reshapes itself too. At the top are the people in the money world--the power brokers. The decisions they make determine how the flow of money progresses in the daily lives throughout the world and it is always ahead of the curve they create. It operates on its own time and pulse. If enough people in these top circles can make more money by creating havoc through protracted warfare and any form of destruction that is the direction the flow of money will go. At this time it is apparent this is the pattern we are in and why some people are predicting that we are headed for the ultimate showdown.

~

As *George Santanya* said *"If you don't know past history, you are bound to repeat its mistakes." and also "You are known by the company you keep." Generation after generation will continue to reveal 'hidden messages' until all of the truth is out.*

VICE PRESIDENT DICK CHENEY

Consenus: Various sources have said that Dick Cheney was the one that started the Iraq war for Halliburton, the company he formerly managed whose profits rose dramatically during the early years of the war:

38

<u>www.charts.com/companies/HAL/gross profit margin</u>:
Mar. 2005-**11.85**%, Sept. 2005-**14.84%,** Mar. 2006–**26.14%,** Sept. 2006– **28.10%,** Dec. 2006-**27.81%,** Mar. 2008-**21.92.**%, through his last four in office.

Through 2009 profits were in the teens, but **under 20%:**
Mar. 2012-**20.25%**, Jun. 2012-**17.53% 20%**, now Jun 2014-**15.94**%. There is a wealth of information on the Internet re: Dick Cheney, Halliburton and his activities.

<u>www.remembering-why-americans-loathe-dick-cheney-the-atlantic-.com/politics/archives/2011/08</u>

While CEO of Halliburton, Cheney reportedly earned 44 million dollars. To this day he denies any wrong doing. *Coincidence?* The sentiment persists that he should be charged for his many instances of wrongdoing. *It still amazes me that he was able to take all of his papers with him when he left the Vice Presidency. He said that the papers were his.* **Question**: Will these papers ever be returned or gotten back? The papers belong to the U.S. government and should be kept as part of the record of this period in history. If he has nothing to hide, why did he take them with him?

Former Vice President Cheney has his own agenda: Unlike the Budget Chairman Paul Ryan, it is very hard to get a whole lot of concrete information on his activities starting in 1972. ***When he left office, his approval rating stood at a staggeringly low 13%.*** This figure is still very fresh in people's minds and for good reason. He got started in the Nixon Administration under his then boss Donald Rumsfeld and met G. Gordon Libby. From that time on these three (Libby—one of the "plumbers" convicted with Howard Hunt in masterminding the Watergate Scandal) worked together. Libby was Vice President Cheney's chief aide in the G. W. Bush administration.

2016 – In my view, Dick Cheney is one of the most astute attorneys in modern times and why he has been so successful at covering his own tracks. His record suggests that his self-interest are always first. Given his history, one has to question his motives.

~

A paper trail no longer exists, but the electric trail has taken its place. Someone will find it.

~

www.washingpost.com/ **Bush Began to Plan War three months after 9/11,**

NOTE: This is General Powell's view of that time only. He has always served honorably and should always be held in the highest esteem.

Secretary of State Collin Powell felt "Cheney and his allies - Chief Aide G. Gordon "Scooter" Libby (this is the same "Scooter" Libby as above), Deputy Defense Secretary Paul D. Wolfowitz, an Undersecretary of Defense for Policy, Douglas J. Feith and what Powell called Feith's "Gestapo" tactics and what amounted to a separate government. The Vice President, for his part believed that he (Powell) was mainly concerned with his own popularity…and "always has major reservations about what we were trying to do." *(Four Star General Colin Powell Secretary of State resigned in November of 2004.)*

NOTE: For those under 55-60 years, who are not history enthusiasts: (the reference to Colin Powell who is a Four Star retired General) was the first Secretary Of State Colin Powell, Cabinet Member of President George W. Bush's Administration. **Also, I. Lewis "Scooter" Libby is another named used by G. Gordon Libby.**

NOTE: I have included the following people-Karl Rove and G. Gordon Libby, who met during the Nixon administration. They have worked with Dick Cheney since the early 1970's, when they became friends. They have worked very closely ever since. They were a very strong part of Cheney's base and in his Vice

Presidency. **2016** – There are whole libraries of material on the Internet on Cheney, Rove and Libby and this particular period in American history; in my view the very black cloud we have all been under and didn't know or understand or why. *Truth Always Prevails.*

Karl Rove

2016 – Note: Karl Rove has been a great contributor in funding money to campaigns from unknown sources.

www.counterpunch.org./2002/22/01/exposingkarlrove:

Karl Rove worked for Donald (Deep Throat) Segretti, chief of political dirty tricks strategist on behalf of Nixon's 1972 campaign. Rove was an ardent student who could be likened in stripe of the fictional character—Svengali. *"His tracks are hard to follow, because of the wide range of people he worked for and with, before finally becoming Deputy Chief of Staff for George W. Bush.*

His role was that of chief strategist." He stepped down August 31, 2007, citing the need to move on.

http://en.wikipedia.org/wiki/KarlRove

Karl Rove: A transplant to Texas has been in the background since his college days, but in 1969 he started his foray into politics leaving a tawdry trail, as he continued to work at the college level, and had been an early advocate of embroiled with his style of campaigning and was targeted as the "Teacher of Dirty Tricks.'

James Dean, then special counsel to President Nixon, "based on my review of the files*, it appears the Watergate prosecutors were interested in Rove's activities in 1972, but because they had bigger fish to fry, they did not aggressively investigate him."* In September 1973 George H. W. Bush chose him to be chairman of the College Republicans.

Rove continued up the ranks working for George H.W. Bush and met George W. Bush, when Senior George H.W. Bush asked him to deliver car keys to George W. It was the first time the two had met and made an instant connection…" **Re G.W. - Rove – "a huge amount of charisma, Swagger …you know, WOW!"**

From 1977-1991, he continued working in the background and "…had worked on hundreds of races, where he had great success winning a total of 34 races."

But his whole history shows he didn't play a fair game and continued being on the side, but always managed to pull through.

He and the **Koch brothers** worked together and that fell apart, and now he and the **Koch's** are on the opposite side of the fence. Having spent so much time at all levels of the RNC he has a very broad range of contacts. Another note of interest is the fact that during the last election *he out-raised the Koch brothers, by 30 million dollars; 270 million Koch's – over 300 million, Rove. (That's a major feat.)*

http://en.wikepedia.org.wiki/lewis_libby
The above website has the nefarious history of G. Gordon Libby on the Internet. His history covers eight pages. He and Karl Rove seem to have been cut from the same cloth. Most of his career as a lawyer is mixed. He tended to be on the wrong side of the law.

"In relation to the outing of an undercover agent Valerie Plame, on October 28, 2005, as a result of the CIA leak grand jury investigation…, Libby was indicted on five counts of obstruction of justice, two counts of making false statements and two counts of perjury in his testimony before the grand jury…"

"In June 2007, he was sentenced to 30 months in prison and fined $250,000 dollars… On July 2, 2007, Bush commuted Libby's sentence… There was criticism of his decision: "We can't find any cases, certainly in the last half-century, where the President commuted a sentence before it had even started to be served…."

Former Senator Newt Gringrich's shows, his history is a long, manipulative one and very informative. He is a supporter of Donald Trump.

2016 – The below was written in the 2014 edition. As more is revealed the following sure points a smoking gun at Newt Gingrich.

Newt Gingrich www.thenation.com/article/165938/how-newt-gingrich-crippled–congress.
Another to add to the list is this wily politician. "I spent 16 years building a majority in the House for the first time since 1954." Also this: "I am trying to effect a change so large that the people who would be hurt by the change, the liberal Democratic machine" will fight it, Gingrich explained. And change it he did. He is said to be the founder of obstructionism and considers this as a major asset.

- In 1995 and 1996, Gingrich took government shutdowns to a new level.
- Spending for 'earmarks' doubled during his watch, from $7.8 billion in 1994 to $14.5 billion in 1997.
- Senator John McCain (R) AZ said… "earmarks led directly to the Abramoff scandal."
- Maneuvered and consolidated power…so that the Speaker could appoint key committee chairmanships.
- Started the Congressional three day work week. (So the three day work week has been in effect for 17-18 years)
- *And Gingrich made winning*, rather than good governance, *the chief currency of success.*

His latest is a recently founded super PAC "Committee for America" to raise money for both his failed presidential campaign and to raise money **for American Legacy Political Action Committee (ALPAC)**—sounds like a pattern close to **ALEC** if you ask me.

THE TEA PARTY

Contributing to the anger felt in the country today has been heightened by decisions of the Supreme Court in favor of Big Business. Five on this Court clearly side with the money interests. They are Chief Justice John G Roberts, Anthony Kennedy, Antonio Scalia, Samuel A. Alito, and Clarence Thomas. It is time for a major change on the Supreme Court, too.

NOTE: Binding regulations for the financial industry are still not in place, even though the Federal Reserve has declared, banking now has to have assets equal to what monies they have out as working capital. This step, while in the right direction, still doesn't guarantee that there will never be another meltdown. Do you think that we are going to be asked to pay for another bailout?

THE TEA PARTY

Def: caucus – may be an openly organized tendency or political faction within the group.

Def: political party – is an organization which seeks to achieve goals common to its members. (taken from the political pages re: these subjects).

The top story today is the one about the IRS targeting Tea Party members. This is a new one. I have never thought the day would come that a "Non-Profit" organization, whose express purpose is to impose their way (tear down) the government,t and then use this tax free money they have raised for the express purpose, to fund people now in office, and to guide legislation along their OWN lines.

The Democratic and Republican parties do not operate under the NON-PROFIT status. **So how and why is the Tea Party allowed to do it?**

By filing their caucus as non-profit, the **TEA PARTY** has side-stepped the regulations governing political parties. This non- profit status for a group whose sole purpose is to influence members of Congress to vote their way, is *completely out of the realm of* what Democracy is all about and absolutely functions as a third party. *They have hijacked the Republican Party.*

It is the way that the House of Representatives Tea Party members and those that support them have subverted our government. The question is: **#1: Why have they been allowed to continue? #2: Why haven't the majority of members of the House of Representatives, who do not adhere to the policies of the TEA PARTY raised a red flag?** An investigation should be started immediately and corrective policies be instituted for this to never happen again.

By listing the names of people involved, everyone will be very clear about the origins of this group and a list of its members. In my view the Tea Party Caucus is an *illegitimate, but_legitimately sanctioned, third party* that came into place as a caucus and doesn't have to abide by the rules of our two- party system. Why hasn't this been questioned? It not only operates in the House, (has members in the Senate too) but clearly is a political party.

The Tea Party Caucus is a Congressional caucus of the United States House of Representatives and Senate launched and chaired by Minnesota Congresswoman Michelle Bachmann on July 16, 2010. The idea of a Tea Party Caucus originated from Kentucky Senator Rand Paul when he was campaigning for his current seat. (More machinations from this Koch protégé and ALEC.)

The caucus was approved as an official congressional member organization by the House Administration Committee on July 19, 2010…its first public event was a press conference on the grounds of the U.S. Capitol, on July 21, 2010. Four Senators joined the caucus on January 27, 2011.

All 54 (were 66) members are members of the Republican Party. Three are in leadership positions. Thomas E. Price, (GA) Republican Committee Chair, 7th ranking member; John R. Carter, (TX) Secretary House Republican Conference, 9th ranking member; and Pete Sessions, (TX) National Republican Congressional Committee, 6th ranking member and *Chair of the NRCC from 2008-2012.*

It was during Congressman Sessions' Chairmanship in 2010 that gave approval for the Tea Party Caucus to be formed. Although they deny that the **Koch** brothers are behind their caucus (see above), from the beginning, it was their money that funded them. The "average" Tea Party caucus member received more than $25,000 from the oil and gas industry, compared to about $13,000 for the average House member and $21,500 for the "average House Republican." There wasn't any information about how much the leaders were given. (Is this money reported on their income tax returns?) Besides gas and oil, donations also come from health professionals, retirees, and the real estate industry.

The following is a known list of the members of the Tea Party Caucus.

- Rodney Alexander, Louisiana
- Michele Bachmann, Minnesota, *Chair*
- Joe Barton, Texas
- Gus Bilirakis, Florida
- Rob Bishop, Utah
- Diane Black, Tennessee
- Michael C. Burgess, Texas
- Paul Broun, Georgia
- John Carter, Texas
- Bill Cassidy, Louisiana
- Howard Coble, North Carolina
- Mike Coffman, Colorado
- Ander Crenshaw, Florida
- John Culberson, Texas
- Jeff Duncan, South Carolina

- Blake Farenthold, Texas
- Stephen Fincher, Tennessee
- John Fleming, Louisiana
- Trent Franks, Arizona
- Phil Gingrey, Georgia
- Louie Gohmert, Texas
- Vicky Hartzler, Missouri
- Tim Huelskamp, Kansas
- Lynn Jenkins, Kansas
- Steve King, Iowa
- Doug Lamborn, Colorado
- Blaine Luetkemeyer, Missouri
- Kenny Marchant, Texas
- Tom McClintock, California
- David McKinley, West Virginia
- Gary Miller, California
- Mick Mulvaney, South Carolina
- Randy Neugebauer, Texas
- Rich Nugent, Florida
- Steven Palazzo, Mississippi
- Steve Pearce, New Mexico
- Ted Poe, Texas
- Tom Price, Georgia
- Phil Roe, Tennessee
- Dennis Ross, Florida
- Ed Royce, California
- Steve Scalise, Louisiana
- Pete Sessions, Texas
- Adrian Smith, Nebraska
- Lamar S. Smith, Texas
- Tim Walberg, Michigan
- Lynn Westmoreland, Georgia
- Joe Wilson, South Carolina

Members of Senate Caucus

- Mike Lee, Utah
- Jerry Moran, Kansas
- Rand Paul, Kentucky
- Tim Scott, South Carolina
- Ted Cruz, Texas
- Rick Santorum. Pennsylvania
- Marco Rubio, Florida

Governors
- Scott Walker, Wisconsin
- Rick Perry, Texas
- Rick Scott, Florida - #1 with NRA
- Paul Le Page, Maine
- Rick Snyder, Michigan
- Brian Sandavol, Nevada
- Susana Martinez, New Mexico
- Tom Corbett, Pennsylvania

2016 – The above are a few that I was able to find. I have no doubt that they are just the tip of a very large iceberg.

NOTE: Because this information is dated, be sure to check if your elected leaders belong to the NRA and Tea Party. Seven of the above Governors belong to both groups; Brian Sandavol appears to be straddling the fence with the NRA. These governors will drastically change the laws in your state and make the fight all the harder to clean this nest out by taking orders from the above groups and their legal arms—**ALEC—NRA**.

September 17, 2013 – In a news clip on the Internet re: the Budget: *Tea Party Caucus holds Boehner to shut down the government if Obamacare is not taken off the table*

THE 2008 MELTDOWN

The CITIZENS of the United States <u>must</u> effectively control the mighty commercial forces which they themselves have called into being.

President Franklin D Roosevelt
32nd President of the United States

Gold is a living god, and rules in scorn
All earthly things but virtue.

Percy Bysshe Shelly
"Rosaline and Helen" (1818)

The first four pages of this essay is in very small print written by **"Judge Jed S. Rakoff, U.S. District Judge for the Southern District of New York**, the nerve center of the financial world." The whole article is 76 pages.

Starting with his first question "Who was to blame? Was it simply a result of negligence, of the kind of inordinate risk-taking commonly called a "bubble," of an imprudent but innocent failure to maintain adequate reserves for a rainy day? Or was it the result, at least in part, of fraudulent practices, of dubious mortgages portrayed as sound risks and packaged into ever more esoteric financial instruments, the fundamental weaknesses of which were intentionally obscured?"

Judge Rakoff acknowledges that if the financial crisis were the product of mere negligence, then prosecution of corporate executives would simply be scapegoating of the worst kind. But if the evidence points to intentional fraud, that is exactly the type of conduct the Justice Department is designed to confront and its failure to do so a travesty of justice in its own right.

"But if, by contrast, the Great Recession was in material part of the product of intentional fraud, *the failure to prosecute those responsible must be judged one of the most egregious failures of the criminal justice system in many years.* Indeed, it would stand in striking contrast to the increased success that federal prosecutors have had over the past fifty years or so in bringing to justice even the highest-level figures who orchestrated mammoth frauds."

At the end of these four pages are some of the thoughts from the author – Dartagnan Daily Kos member – first and last of the final statement:

"The effects of this artificial, completely avoidable cataclysm on the entire world were so profound, and the consequences so radical, the true ends will likely not manifest themselves for decades…"

NOTE: ATTORNEY GERNERAL Eric Holder: I think the right decision was made, not to prosecute. This scandal affects everyone in office at that time, if not directly by association, by who knew what. Charges and counter-charges would continue to surface with lawsuits to follow. A clear decision could never be obtained in this climate and trials would be unending.

THE BUDGET

2016 – 5/16 www.nytimes.com/topic/organization/congressional-budget-office. House Republicans in Federal Court last week; if upheld on appeal, it would block the Administration from reimbursing discounts for low income people.

http://thehill.com/on-the-money/budget/ **August 29, 2013**

"White House, Senate GOP debt talks on the rocks after meeting. The sides remain "far apart" on the scope of the problem and size of a solution…" a White House official indicated after the meeting ended that the stumbling block remained the issue of raising taxes to cut the deficit. **(The current rating for this Congress is 19%.)**

http://budget.house.gov/about/

Note: This website has a nine page report: HOUSE OF REPRESENTATIVES – COMMITTEE ON THE BUDGET –

The Constitution Gives Congress Power of the Purse to the Budget Committee; that is the power to spend, collect revenue, and borrow. *It does not, however, establish procedures by which Congress must consider budget-related legislation.* Instead, it states that each chamber may, "determine the Rules of its Proceedings."

Over time, Congress has therefore developed various rules and practices to govern consideration of budgetary legislation. The composition of the Budget Committee is then cited for the number from each committee that will serve on the Budget Committee. **The original number was 23; over time it has evolved to 39.**

NOTE: *The number of service terms, in successive Congresses is also spelled out...both Democrats and Republicans designate the Budget Committee as a non-exclusive committee in general. (This means besides the House rule restricting any Member from serving on more than two standing committees, fewer restrictions apply to Budget Committee members regarding committee assignments.)*

BUDGET PROCESS REFORM: NOTE: Since 1995, House Rules have provided that the Budget Committee shall have jurisdiction over the budget process generally. ...In addition to creating the House and Senate Budget Committees, the Budget Act also established the Congressional Budget Office in 1974. House rules state that the Budget Committee shall be responsible for Congressional Budget Office functions and duties. The Budget Committee plays a role in the selection of the Director of the Congressional Budget Office.*

*This doesn't make sense; the oversight Director is appointed by the Budget Committee. And who has the final say—the Budget Chairman. Clearly, something is VERY WRONG with this picture.

RED FLAG*: Provisions...grant the Budget Chairman Paul Ryan (not the entire Budget Committee) the authority to revise or adjust budget levels and other matters included in the annual budget resolution in certain circumstances. **This makes him a virtual KINGPIN of the budget process.** No wonder the Budget Chairman, Paul Ryan, has his finger in so many pies—there is nothing to stop him—apparently even Speaker Boehner (and I surmise from the stance he has taken for some time now, that he is turning a blind eye? Or couldn't be happier; this is quite a fix.)* Do I have this all wrong? *I certainly hope so. I know that I will be informed.*

(Reminder: This is the Chairman of the Committee, that provides the funds to run the national government and all programs affecting the lives of all Americans.)

www.politico.com/story/ - **August 9, 2013 Eric Cantor, Paul Ryan Head Koch summit.** Representative Paul Ryan, House

Majority Leader Eric Cantor and New Mexico Governor Susana Martinez secretly spoke to wealthy donors at the Koch brothers' recently concluded summer gathering on the outskirts of Albuquerque... there is a list of many recognizable names in attendance. *Cantor and Ryan are both in the middle of nearly every piece of legislation that crosses the House floor...* Now that Eric Cantor has been voted out of office, will this help to change the picture? And what will Paul Ryan do without his sidekick?

NOTE: Paul Ryan, the budget Chairman...has collected millions of dollars from individuals and groups (with his stance to privatize Social Security and reform *Medicaid and Medicare – Industrialists Charles and David Koch.)*

When the city of Kenosha, Wisconsin was preparing to *formally petition Congress to take the necessary action to get corporate money out of politics* and restore grass roots democracy their Congress man Paul Ryan was secretly meeting with the Koch brothers to plot election strategies nad policy agendas.

Sixteen states and roughly 500 communities have petitioned Congress to support a CONSTITUONAL ADMENDMENT to restore to the people... by placing limits and on the influence of big money especially cooperate money in American politics.

The official calls from states across the country...come in response to the high court's decision to remove restrictions on cooperate spending to buy elections, which capped a series of rulings that undermined limits on the power of wealthy Americans to dominate the political and governing processes of the nation, with unprecedented infusions of campaign money.

2016 – June, 2013, Supreme Court decision to enact Citizens United.

*John Nichols, a Washington correspondent for The Nation is and associate editor of The Capital Times in Madison, Wisconsin. He has written several books, the latest: *The "S" Word: A Short*

History of an American Tradition. He is also, co-founder of the media reform organization Free Press.

Note: I hope the above information will encourage immediate, strong debate for the merits of a constitutional amendment. I would also include the need to have revised rules for the Budget Committee. (See Banking – page 114.)

www.pressherald.com/politics/critics-call-pension-plan-for-congress-too-generous

After retiring from a 36-year career, the U.S. House of Representative, Norm Dicks (Democrat), has no doubt that he is worth every penny of his new pension of $7,365.82 per month; gross amount $107, 266 a year.

Dicks, who is now working as a consultant with defense companies, is among a handful of departing members of Congress who are eligible for six-figure pensions...about 75 new retireeswill add to the estimated $28 million in yearly pensions. Florida Republican Rich Nugent said Congress should at least allow members to opt out of the pension system. "Personally, I don't believe we should be there 30 to 40 years."

Question: *What about former members of Congress working as consultants for defense companies or any other. That has contracts with the government, another form of double dipping? Look for more examples to be published – they help tell the tale of how embedded graft is accepted in government today.*

As of October 2011, 495 retired members of Congress were drawing pensions under the different plans...**not having to disclose specific information, became effective with the Freedom of Information Act, 1980.**

Pete Sepp, Executive Vice President of the National Taxpayers Union...on average Congress' pension systems cost $25 million to $30 million per year...depending on length of service.

Most members of Congress keep their tax returns secret. The House Minority Leader Nancy Pelosi was emphatic. Mitt Romney's refusal to release more than two years of his personal tax returns, she said, makes him unfit to win confirmations as a member of the President's Cabinet, let alone to hold the high office…yet she will not provide hers.

In fact, only 15 members in Congress offered to submit their tax returns. I do not imagine any one of the Democrats or Republicans among the 261 millionaires in Congress is part of these 15. The other position that I don't understand is that I don't know if any of the millionaires of Congress agree to have their taxes raised. All of them have been amazingly quiet on this issue.

www.legistorm.com/member/79/

Leadership in both House and Senate; total salaries from January 2001 to March 31, 2013:

Senate Majority Leader	$ 193,400
Total # employees – 159	$16,065,239
Senate Minority Leader	$ 193,400
Total # employees*	?
Speaker of the House	$ 223,000
Total # employees – 140	$10,978,853
House Majority Leader	$ 193,400
Total # employees*	?
House Minority Leader	$ 193,400
Total # employees – 105	$12,065,239
Senate Minority Leader*	
Est. # employees – 100	$ 9,500,000
House Majority Leader*	
Est. # employees – 100	$ 9,500,000
Total	$59,105,931

Offices – for 609 employees from 10/01/2000 – 6/20/2103. Note: This website did not provide information for the Senate Minority Leader, Mitch McConnell (R) or for the House Majority Leader, Eric Cantor (R).

www.usovinfo.com/about

The ten top millionaires total Worth:

> Low -- $1,016,300,000,000
> High -- $2,812,500,000,000

Ten people in Congress worth nearly 3 TRILLION DOLLARS.

www.huffingtionpost.com/2013/03/29/walmart-ceo-pay

WalMart's CEO paid 1,034 times more than the median WalMart worker; PayScale.

Meet Mike Duke, King of the CEO-to-worker pay ratio:

Duke, who raked in $23,150,000 last year, contended in December, that the retail giant pays "competitive wages". Half of WalMart's workers made less than $22,400 in 2012, according to PayScale which is below the poverty level for a family of four.

Raising the minimum wage for all working people should be at the $10.10 recommended by the President in his State of the Union Address, when he announced he would seek raising the minimum wage for all government workers.

POLITICS AND VALUES

My question is whether
can we overcome the
arrogance of power.

Senator J. William Fulbright
– Arkansas 1945-1975

"Those how *desire to* give up Freedom
in order to gain security will not have,
nor do they deserve either one.

Benjamin Franklin

Time Warp - The following is very interesting and so I am beginning this section on political times in the past. You will see that nothing in Republican priorities has changed. The following are from early times.

The following was written by **Vice President John Adams** taken from a series of articles to be published in the *Gazette of the United States,* in **1790:**

(The)...major thought was the imperfectability of man... "ambition, jealousy, greed, envy, vanity: mankind would never and could never rid itself of these attributes. The only way man could be forced to behave himself was by a government of laws which took into account these weaknesses and found a means to contain them. He did not believe that Utopia could be achieved on earth, neither did he believe that, as the Declaration of Independence stated, "All men are created equal." *The most any government could do was give people the opportunity to be free and equal; and further on...to defend legislators from themselves."*

I am also including the following excerpts, as they not only reflect what can and did happen in the Presidency, but also can be applied to certain people in Congress who are obsessed with their positions.

Also a reminder: the Republican Party has not changed its message as long as I have been on this earth.

In off-year elections the Republicans, (mine), "...being out of office for thirteen years, they swept the off-year elections...they block...public housing, Social Security extension, anti-lynching law, anti-poll tax law, the Fair Employment Practices Commission, aid to education, and his anti-inflation program. It passed a tax bill favoring the rich, yet over another Presidential veto."

When was this, you ask? In the off-year elections in 1945; 68 years ago, during President Truman's terms in office.
Following are some of the items that are pertinent because of their relevance to this whole section. They are in somewhat random order.

The following are from the 4th edition of:

THE PRESIDENTIAL CHARACTER – James David Barber
Referring to President Reagan commenting the he "would stick to the script" after causing many heads to shake… was followed in the book with this observation: The Presidency is of necessity a performance… **"The dark side of power and drama is to overwhelm reason: The lure of illusion, the fracturing of logic, the collapse of political conversation. The dark side is the drift into the swamp of fantasy and on over into the brink of disaster. Drama offers interest, but it risks political insanity. <u>That process begins with contempt for the facts."</u>**

Mr. Barber: "…a debate should be concentrated on one question for a significant period of time, so that logic and evidence may be brought forth for citizens to evaluate the thinking of a candidate regarding one major challenge."

<u>Re: The Supreme Court:</u> "It is even conceivable that the Supreme Court, and the whole legal structure it stands on, will learn how to break through the toils of complexity that now threaten the very

THE PENTAGON
www.reuters.com/article/2013/11/18/us-usa-pentagon-wast-specialreport-idUSBRE... **Scott J. Palrow**

"Special Report" the Pentagon's doctored ledgers conceal epic waste.
This recent twelve page report is another **MUST READ. "…**As the use of plugs indicates, pay errors are only a small part of the s-um that annually disappear into the vast bureaucracy that **manages more than half of all annual government outlays approved by Congress. The Defense Department's 2012 budget totaled $565.8 billion, more than the annual defense budgets of the next 10 largest military spenders, combined…"**

Paul Szoldra

In this article, the 17 agencies *include five that were established during the President G. W. Bush Administration including:*

- 1) National Reconnaissance – "Office of the Director" Where all intelligence should come together for delivery to the President - 2004. Specifics of office are unknown but the aggregate amount is $48 billion.
- 2) "Surprisingly" Department of Treasury – Combat terrorism and *illicit financial transactions – 2004.*
- 3) National Geo-Spatial Intelligence Agency – 2005; Budget classified; employs approximately 14,500.
- 4) FBI – National Security Branch – 2005; Budget **$8.1 billion** in 2012 which included $119 million "...to enhance counter terrorism, computer intrusion and other programs." Why didn't they know about Eric Snowden?
- *Regular budget for the Bureau was another $8.12 billion.* The following are my observations:

The standard agencies are: CIA, NSA, State Department – Bureau of Intelligence, Air Force Intelligence, Army Intelligence, Coast Guard Intelligence, Drug Enforcement Agency, Marine Corps Intelligence Activity, National Geo-Spatial Agency, Naval Intelligence, and Homeland Security.

It appears that the following are a duplication of efforts:

State Department of Intelligence and Research.
Why can't research be included in the Intelligence Department?

FBI National Security Branch (2005)
This department of the FBI conflicts with Homeland Security.

Army Intelligence and Security Communications and the **National Geo-Spatial Intelligence Agency (2005),** overlap in their missions according to the statements. **Army Intelligence Mission:**

C4ISR – Command, Control, Communications, Computers, Intelligence, Surveillance, and Reconnaissance.

Department of Energy (2004) The NSA is the largest agency in the world. Why can't the Department of Energy get a report from them?*

*Budget unknown – "…like other government budgets, activity is not specifically mentioned, although it may fall under "Atomic Energy Defense Activities" which had a total budget of $16 billion in 2012." It appears to me Atomic Energy does not come under the Department of Energy.

Department of the Treasury (2004) Same as above.

The above National Reconnaissance office had the following information: Two main missions: *"to lead intelligence integration and forge an intelligence communication that delivers the most insightful intelligence possible; where all intelligence should come together for delivery to the President."* I thought this was the responsibility of the appointed Cabinet members. Does this department have more stature than all of the rest? If so, why is the NSA the largest in the world? Isn't a direct report from them sufficient?

It is interesting that all of these offices were established in the period from 9/11 and during the wars in the Middle East. Now that we are in another phase, maybe it is possible to reduce the size of the intelligence community by eliminating these agencies.

The following from the Business Insiders 12 page report **certainly** supports the Reuters report.

BONUS: The Intelligence community has rapidly expanded since 9/11.
"…A ground breaking investigation from the Washington Post found some daunting figures: 1,271 government organizations and

1,931 private companies working on intelligence; NSA alone contracted 250 companies..."

(A SPECIAL NOTE)
"...One reason why intelligence budgets are marked classified— millions of dollars in so called "ghost money" was paid to foreign governments..."

Why, after six years since the major financial meltdown of 2008 are some people in the money industry predicting another meltdown within five years or sooner? Median CEO Pay climbs to $9.7M... a 6.5% increase from a year earlier... CEO pay, which fell two years straight during the Great Recession, but rose 24% in 2010 and 6% in 2011, has never been higher.

NOTE: The "Dark Side of Trading" Anita Kumar - McClatchy Newspapers

"Wall Street is embracing its dark side. As the stock market has continued to climb, trading has increasingly migrated from established bourses like the New York Stock Exchange to private platforms, including dark pools that are largely hidden from public view. The shift is helping big traders hide what they are doing in the markets and regulators are worried that the development could obscure the true prices of stocks and scare away ordinary investors. movement, underway for several years, has gathered force. Recently the trend has bucked the government's broad effort to move more of the financial industry out of the back rooms and into the light. The increasing fuzziness of stock trading in the United States, long the most transparent place in the financial world, is troubling for investors and regulators. "We have been having a lot of discussions about whether *we are reaching a tipping point between "lit and unlit markets," said Thomas Gira, head of market regulation at the Financial Industry Regulatory Authority."*

In our newspaper *THE OLYMPIAN was* the following:
SEPTEMBER, 2014: Justice Investigating high-speed trading.

"The FBI confirmed this week that it has been investigating high-frequency trading firms for about a year. The Wall Street Journal reported Tuesday that investigators were examining the practice of placing a group of trades and then canceling them to create the false appearance of market activity."

National Security Agency
The following articles may help to shine a light on why some of the deterioration has set into government.

Judge backs NSA data collection – He *says it protects us from terrorism; conflicting rulings likely mean the Supreme Court will get a final say.*

Friday's decision by U.S. District Judge William Pauley in Manhattan diverged from the ruling by another judge this month that questioned the program's constitutionality... Pauley ruled 11 days after U.S. District Judge Richard Leon of Washington D.C. said the "almost Orwellian" NSA program amounted to an "indiscriminate and arbitrary invasion" that was likely unconstitutional...The ACLU said it "was extremely disappointed." Judge Richard Leon was nominated by President G. W. Bush. Judge William Pauley was nominated by President Bill Clinton. It will be interesting to see how this ruling goes. Unfortunately it could have more of a political outcome than a **right one.**

It opens with the following "There is a vast total-information-awareness surveillance network made up of global corporations and subservient (captured) governments engaging in the systematic infiltration and suppression of social justice activist groups. Their main method of control is the implementation of divide-and conquer-strategies, including the breaking into major accounts and obtaining critical private information of investors."

legitimacy of the idea of law itself, and stand as the trusted ultimate guardians of American justice." **2016** - Does this sound like the recent full Court?

Re: The Presidency: "We need Presidents who know how the world works and how Washington works in it. Presidents who have mastered the skills it takes to make the White House an efficient machine for social progress, Presidents who can call up from their own characters the steady, hopeful, insistent reasoning to shape a good life from a mixed society. **(2016) - We yet may find the best Presidents before the great American adventure stops."**

"If you want to study the social and political history of modern times, *study Hell.*"   Thomas Merton

~

WHO GETS THE MOST VALUE
FROM GUN CONTROL

No one denies the right to bear arms;
BUT the line has to be drawn on military and
Multi-purpose assault weapons.

In order to get this issue into focus, the first repeating rotating cannon was the Gattling gun, developed by Dr. Richard Gattling in 1861 and was first used in the Civil War. Automatic hand held guns were not fully developed until World War II. The ultra-sophisticated weapons of today are inventions in the last 50 years.

NRA/GUN CONTROL – Automated weapons were not invented when the Constitution was drawn up. It was not conceivable at that time, that 100 years later, an automated gun would be invented. Guns in the 1700's were single shot. The Constitution is our first resource as to the laws of the land. *The **NRA/GUN** position for everyone to own assault weapons has no legal foundation or merit for their position. All arguments surrounding this issue should be considered null and void.*

The Vice President and CEO of the NRA, Wayne La Pierre stated earlier on television this year that he could guarantee that no gun control measures would be passed through the Congress. The only way he could be so self-assured is because members in both houses of Congress have been convinced *by some means* to vote as directed by the NRA. In view of what is transpiring in other legislation this is another area that needs to be addressed.

Note: *After the Sandy Hook massacre, ABC News reported that of all of the children that are killed by guns in the world, **85% are killed in United States.***

ALERT: The NRA established the Institute for Legislative Action (ILA) in 1975; the same year that ALEC—American Legislative Executive Council was founded by the Koch brothers. The ILA is the legal arm of the NRA. This type of institute was a popular one to start that year.

ABC EVENING NEWS: A news clip was shown of an ATF worker having to search through years and years of paper records to obtain information needed in pending background checks. The idea of establishing a central database of gun transactions has been rejected by lawmakers in *Congress who have sided with the National Rifle Association,* which argues that such a database poses a threat to the Second Amendment.

Law enforcement officials say that in theory, the ATF could take a lead role but are hampered by politically driven laws that make it's job harder and by the ferocity of the gun debate. Frederick H. Bealefeld III, a former police commissioner in Baltimore said: "I think that they've really been muzzled over the last several years, at least from doing their job effectively." The agency has been without a Director for over six years, however has had a permanent Director since June of this year.

Follow up: Also in this news story; ... on the length of time to complete a background check with this old method it takes up to five days to get just one background check out. If the ATF's record keeping were to be put into a computer, it would take just a few hours at the most. Senator Chuck Grassley (R-IA) was questioned re: this process, the Senator said he supports every provision that protects the Second Amendment.

The following is a KEY piece of information, explaining why the people in charge of the agencies mentioned, have taken the course of action they did—they didn't have a choice, because their hands have been tied.

APRIL, 2013: Anita Kumar Reporter – McClatchy Newspapers Headlines this article with "Movement to Hinder Gun Rules, Research a Quiet One."

ALERT: She states, "It's the reason the Centers for Disease Control and Prevention can't research gun violence, The Federal Bureau of Investigation can't use data to detect firearms traffickers and the ***Bureau of Alcohol, Tobacco, Firearms, and Explosives can't require background checks on older guns."

*** *"Since the late 1970's, more than a dozen provisions have been added to must-pass spending bills with no hearings, no debate and no vote in a way that's designed to circumvent the usual legislative process... "It's not well known," said Rep. Mike Quigley, "but this is an inherent problem."*

"It makes enforcement nearly impossible..." Once the so-called riders are in, they are difficult to get out, all but ensuring they remain in, year after year, no matter which party controls the Congress and the White House. "They're trying to say we get a special deal with these riders," **NRA** spokesman Andrew Arulanandam said in an interview. "It's just the way business is done in this town."

http://bluevirginia.us/diary/8333/who-funds-the-nra

Whenever a National Rifle Association spokesman goes on television to claim that the NRA gets its money from its membership in small donations, he is lying through his teeth. *The real money behind the organization is from industries that make and sell guns and ammunition, as well as right-wing wealthy donors from domestic and foreign gun manufactures and other corporations related to the firearms industry through its "corporate outreach program."* *(list to follow.)

NOTE: Those who gave money to the NRA include 22 gun makers, 12 of which manufacture assault rifles and high-capacity ammunition magazine, or sellers. Beretta alone donated one million dollars to the NRA to lobby to overturn gun control laws in the wake of the 2008 Supreme Court decision in the *District of Columbia v. Heller, which eliminated laws against handguns.*

Josh Sugarmann: The Violence Policy Center Executive Director Josh Sugarmann states, "Today's NRA is a virtual subsidiary of the gun industry." While the NRA portrays itself as protecting the freedom of individual gun owners, *"it's actually working to protect*

68

the freedom of the gun industry to manufacture and sell virtually any weapon or accessory..." Further "*Its purpose is to be a front for corporate lobbying, to help legislators who will resist any and all gun regulation, and to strike fear in its members about gun control.*" (Again, shades of 1930's Europe before World War II.)

Meet 34 Corporations That Help Inflate the NRA's Membership – 03/06/2013

www.thinkprogress.org:
The company headquarters should be boycotted. The line is fine here because of all of the innocent workers who will be affected by boycott. The better way is for loyal Americans in the TV and publication industries to start an all-out push to expose the heads of these companies. This technology firm gives a 25% discount for gun clubs and stores buying software systems, a spokeswoman said.

www.thinkprogress.org "We have been a longtime partner of the NRA because we have many clients who are firearm dealers and several who are NRA members. We are a retail software company, and we specialize in many different retail verticals, one of them being firearms. *We offer a discount to NRA members and do not have plans to discontinue our partnership.*"

A software company in this list told **thinkprogress.com,** "that it allows any lawful group to receive a commission if they sign up as *affiliate partners.*" Though the NRA Business Alliance site, identifies them as offering a discount, he explained: "We do not pay any fee to the NRA, and their affiliates do not receive any discount on our software."

The Los Angeles Times reported in January that a global advocacy site is encouraging Facebook users to urge two lodging companies "to get out of bed with the extremist NRA."

www.thinkprogress.org:
We reached out to all of the other companies and the NRA for comment. Representatives from a delivery company, a car

company and an affinity group, all declined to comment on their "proprietary" relationships with the NRA. The others did not respond to inquiries from the group.

Following is a list of the enterprises that are "partners" with the NRA:

- American Cellars Wine Club/Vinesse – Discounted membership in the American Cellars Wine Club.
- Americap – Discounted custom-decorated caps, pistol holsters, clay bags, and apparel.
- Avis/Budget Group – Discounts on Avis and Budget car rentals.
- Best Western – Discounted rates at hotels worldwide.
- Celerant Technology – A 25% discount for gun clubs and stores buying software systems.
- Outdoor Affinity – Discounted telecomm services.
- Payment Alliance International – Discounted credit card processing, especially for gun vendors.
- Rescue 360 – Discounted emergency rescue services.
- SIRVA – Discounted moving services.
- Smartwaiver – Discounted legal waivers.
- Sportsmans Bench Products/ND Industries – Discounted adhesives.
- Staples Advantage (Corporate Express) – Discounted Staples office supplies.
- Starkey Hearing Technologies – Discounted hearing aids.
- TN Marketing L.L.C. – Discounted gun videos.
- TrueCar – Discounts on new and used cars.
- Wild Apricot – Discounted membership and website software.
- Wyndham Hotel Group – Discounts at Days Inn, Howard Johnson, Ramada, Super 8, and other Wyndham hotel chains.

The **Los Angeles Times** reported in January that the global advocacy site www.avaaz.org is encouraging Facebook users to rge

Best Western and Wyndham "to get out of bed with the extremist NRA."

www.thinkprogress.org reached out to all of the other companies and the NRA for comment. Representatives for FedEx, Hertz and Lockton Affinity declined to comment on their "proprietary" relationships with the NRA. The others did not respond to inquiries by press time."

The following is a list of twitter handles of U.S. Senators who rejected a bipartisan compromise amendment to expand gun background checks. They voted no on the measure, excluding Senate Majority Leader Harry Reid (D-Nevada) who voted against the amendment on procedural grounds.

- Sen.LamarAlexander(R-Tenn.) @SenAlexander
- Sen. Kelly Ayotte (R-N.H.) - @KellyAyotte
- Sen.JohnBarrasso(R-Wyo.) @SenJohnBarrasso
- Sen. Max Baucus (D-Mont.) - @MaxBaucus
- Sen. Mark Begich (D-Alaska) - @SenatorBegich
- Sen. Roy Blunt (R-Mo.) - @RoyBlunt
- Sen. John Boozman (R-Ark.) - @JohnBoozman
- Sen. Richard Burr (R-N.C.) - @SenatorBurr
- Sen.SaxbyChambliss(R-Ga.)@SaxbyChambliss
- Sen. Dan Coats (R-Ind.) - @SenDanCoats
- Sen. Tom Coburn (R-Okla.) - @TomCoburn
- Sen.Thad Cochran (R-Ms) - @SenThadCochran
- Sen. Bob Corker (R-Tenn.) - @SenBobCorker
- Sen. Jon Comyn (R-Texas) - @JohnComyn
- Sen. Mike Crapo (R-Idaho) - @MikeCrapo
- Sen. Ted Cruz (R-Texas) - @SenTedCruz
- Sen. Mike Enzi (R-Wyo.) – @SenatorEnzi
- Sen. Deb Fischer (R-Neb.) - @SenatorFischer
- Sen. Jeff Flake (R-Ariz.) - @JeffFlake
- Sen. Lindsey Graham (R-S.C.) - @GrahamBlog
- Sen.ChuckGrassley(R-Iowa) - @ChuckGrassley
- Sen. Orrin Hatch (R-Utah) - @SenOrrinHatch

- Sen.HeidiHeitkamp(D-N.D.) @SenatorHeitkamp
- Sen. Dean Heller (R-Nev.) - @SenDeanHeller
- Sen.John Hoeven (R-N.D.) - @SenJohnHoeven
- Sen. James Inhofe (R-Okla.) - @JimInhofe
- Sen.Johnny Isakson (R-Ga.) - @SenatorIsakson
- Sen. Mike Johanns (R-Neb.) - @Mike Johanns
- Sen. Ron Johnson (R-Wis.) - @SenRonJohnson
- Sen. Mike Lee (R-Utah) - @SenMikeLee
- Sen.MitchMcConnell(R-Ky.)- @McConnellPress
- Sen. Jerry Moran (R-Kan.) - @JerryMoran
- Sen.LisaMurkowski(R-Alaska) - @lisamurkowski
- Sen. Rand Paul (R-Ky.) - @SenRandPaul
- Sen. RobPortman (R-Ohio) - @SenRobportman
- Sen. Mark Pryor (D-Ark.) - @SenMarkPryor
- Sen. Jim Risch (R-Idaho) - @SenatorRisch
- Sen. Pat Roberts (R-Kan.) - @SenPatRoberts
- Sen. Marc Rubio (R-Fla.) - @SenMarcrubio
- Sen. Tim Scott (R-S.C.) - @SenatorTimScott
- Sen. Jeff Sessions (R-Ala.) - @SenatorSessions
- Sen.RichardShelby(R-Ala.) - @SenShelbyPress
- Sen. John Thune (R-S.D.) - @SenJohnThune
- Sen. David Vitter (R-La.) -@DavidVitter
- Sen. Roger Wicker (R-Miss.) - @SenatorWicker

NOTE: A list of the people in the House of Representatives who voted in favor of the NRA is not available.

Bob Menendez (NJ)	Mary Landrieu (LA)
Kirsten Gillibrand (NY)	Mark Begich (AK)
Mark Pryor (AR)	Chris Coons (DE)
Mark Warner (VA)	Bob Casey (PA)
Chuck Schumer (NY)	Ben Cardin (MD)
Dick Blumenthal (CT)	Chris Coons (DE)

AND: **Senator Diane Feinstein, Chair of the Senate Select Committee on Intelligence issued a statement recently saying**

that there is no way that then Secretary of State Hillary Clinton can be held responsible for Benghazi and not to make this a political issue.

PART TWO

POLITICAL LIFE AND
LOSS OF POWER

Power must never be trusted without a check.

John Adams – Second President of
the United States

There is higher law than government.
That's the law of conscience.

Stokely Carmicheal

NOTE: Our state and local governments are based on our national government. On all levels, our elected representatives take the following Oath of Office, stating that they will uphold the principles set forth in our Constitution.

Oath of Office

"I do solemnly swear (or affirm) that I will support and defend the Constitution of the United States against all enemies, foreign and domestic; that I will bear true faith and allegiance to the same; that I take this obligation freely, without any mental reservation or purpose of evasion; and that I well and will faithfully discharge the duties of the office on which I am about to enter. So help me God."

We the people vote for candidates that we think best represent our views. In truth, we know very little about these people and we *trust* those who are schooled in government proceedings to give us accurate information. However, human nature being what it is, not all people have our best interests at heart. Graft and corruption are bound to make inroads into the best of people for their personal gain.

But when enough evidence surfaces to show that this CLIMATE OF SELF-WILL takes precedence over the will of the people, then **"We The People"** must stand up and take the steps necessary to regain the balance needed to keep the Ship of State on course; to protect the very life of freedom that we enjoy, as guaranteed by our Constitution. This is a part of our history and history is replete with

I am asking everyone to think of another piece to add to this puzzle. That way we will be able to make the connections and clean this current nest out. More nests will follow. Democracy seems to be a magnet for these types.

~

CONGRESSIONAL BENEFITS

Politicians are the only people in the world who **Create Problems** *and then campaign against them." –* **PAY AND PERQUISITES OF CONGRESS**

Our public and political life here in America is all encompassing. We all live by the laws and regulations that are set in our nation's Capital. We depend on these lawmakers and their wisdom to make laws for all of us to live by.

An example of what is happening today was depicted by a political cartoonist (I couldn't read the person's name). Last spring, a cruise ship was broken down in the middle of the ocean with a ship full of passengers on vacation. They were stranded for several days and far enough out in the ocean that they couldn't be taken to shore. All of the systems of the ship had failed; no fresh water, air conditioning, food storage and most importantly, the bathrooms, no showers, spoiled food and all sanitation were raising quite a stench. The ship had to be pulled back to port by tugboats.

Several days later after finally reaching port, the weary passengers were upset and demanding the company be held responsible for putting people at risk because of mismanagement at many levels. People were adamant that action be taken by the company to shake up their whole chain of command. *It sounds like this is the perfect metaphor for Congress.*

Politics from time on end, stirs men in a way that no other subject has the power to do. This is the way our politics are today; they are right down dirty, scathing, and costly with the attitude that I am going to win control, no matter what the cost, or at whose expense, *especially the honest, hard-working Americans who voted them into office.*

It is not a stretch to say there are people in both houses of Congress who have served so long that their skills are now less sharp than they were when first elected, and it is time for them to be retired. There are also many in the current Congress whose motives are

76

highly questionable. It is up to us, we citizens during the election cycles, to determine the qualifications of those running for office, to have the credentials and knowledge of their responsibilities to their constituencies. Going on the Internet is the quickest way to gain information to help you make highly considered choices.

We have come to a major pivotal point at this time in our history. Are we to be held hostage by a few who have vowed to tear down our form of government or will we make this off-year election, 2014, the turning of the tide in regaining integrity, ethics and moral values—now completely displaced in Congress?

Why Vote - The following is a very clear illustration showing every vote counts.

In the mid-1970's my husband belonged to one of the trade unions. It was time for the members to elect a new General Manager. Over 26,000 votes were cast. The new manager won, by **9** votes. The International office was called in to recount the votes. **The final count was 11 votes for the new manager.**

Politics from time on end, stirs men in a way that no other subject has the power to do. This is the way our politics are today; they are right down dirty, scathing, and costly with the attitude that I am going to win control, no matter what the cost, or at whose expense, *especially the honest, hard-working Americans who voted them into office.*

Starting with the leadership, I have written about the issues that have to be dealt with NOW. In order to get back on course, all disruptive patterns and personalities need to be dealt with FIRST. People that are appointed to leadership positions, from both parties, should have a bi-partisan meeting to establish ground rules that all can abide by in both Houses of Congress.

Until sound ground rules are established we will continue to flounder, like the years since 9/11/2001.

Please! – take this message seriously.

PLEASE!
GO TO THE POLLS THIS NOVEMBER
AND VOTE

AND
REMEMBER:
NO VOTE – NO VOICE
AND
NO COMPLAINTS

PENSIONS AND PAYROLLS
AND CUTS

liven' large, livin' large…

2016 – I have not changed any of this information, nor have I checked to see what the current status is today. I feel that the numbers are higher. What do you think?

www.presshearld.com/politics/critics-call-pension-plan-for-congress-too-generous

After retiring from a 36-year career, the U.S. House of **Representative Norm Dicks, WA (Democrat)** has no doubt that he is worth every penny of his new pension of $7,365.82 per month; gross amount $107,268 a year.

Dicks, who is now working as a consultant with defense companies, is among a handful of departing members of Congress who are eligible for six-figure pensions... about 75 new retirees will add to the estimated $28 million in yearly pensions. Florida Republican Rich Nugent said Congress should at least allow members to opt out of the pension system... "Personally, I don't believe we should be there 30 to 40 years."

Question: What about former members of Congress, working as consultants for defense companies or any other company that has contracts with the government; another form of double or triple dipping? Look for more examples to be published -- they help tell the tale of how embedded graft is accepted in government today.

As of October 2011, 495 retired members of Congress were drawing pensions under the different plans...**not having to disclose specific information became effective with the Freedom of Information Act, 1980.**
Pete Sepp, Executive Vice President of the National Taxpayers Union...on average Congress' pension systems **cost $25 million to $30 million per year**...depending on length of service.

www.mcclatchydc.com/2012/07/18/most-members-of-Congress-keep
Most Members of Congress keep their tax returns secret. The House Minority Leader Nancy Pelosi was emphatic about Mitt Romney's

refusal to release more than two years of his personal tax returns,. She said, it makes him unfit to win confirmation as a member of the President's Cabinet, let alone to hold the high office…yet she won't provide hers.

In fact only 15 members in Congress offered to submit their tax returns. I don't imagine any one of the Democrats or Republicans among the 261 millionaires in Congress is part of these 15. The other position that I don't understand; I don't know if any of the millionaires in Congress agree to have their taxes raised. All of them have been amazingly quiet on this issue. ???

www.legistorm.com/member/

Leadership in Both Houses, total salaries from January 2001 – March 31, 2013.

Senate Majority Leader	$	193,400.00
Total # employees -159	$16,065,239.00	
.Senate Minority Leader –	$	193,400.00
Total # of employees*	?	
Speaker of the House –	$	223,000.00
Total # of employees–140	$10,978,853.00	
House Majority Leader – *	$	193,400.00
Total # of employees --	?	
House Minority Leader	$	193,400.00
Total # of employees – 105 --	$12,065,239.00	
*Senate Minority Leader --		
Est. # of employees – 100 --	$ 9,500,000.00	
*House Majority Leader --		
Est. # of employees – 100 --	$ 9,500,000.00	
Total	$59,105,931.00	

In four offices - for 609 employees from 10/01/2000-6/30/2013 - NOTE: this website did not provide information for the Senate Minority Leader Mitch McConnell or for the House Majority Leader Eric Cantor. *I **Find this very interesting.***

The Ten Top Millionaires Total Worth -
> Low - $1,016,300,000.000
> High - $ 2,812,500,000.000

Ten people in Congress are worth nearly three (3) TRILLION DOLLARS.

WalMart's CEO Paid 1,034 times more than the Median WalMart Worker: PayScale

Meet Mike Duke, king of the CEO-to-worker pay ratio:
Duke, who raked in $23,150,000 last year, contended in December, that the retail giant pays "competitive wages." Half of WalMart's workers made less than $22,400 in 2012, according to Pay Scale which is below poverty level for a family of four.

House Votes To REVERSE No Child Left Behind.
July 20, 2013 – Lyndsey Layton - The Washington Post

House Republicans passed a bill Friday to reduce the federal role in public education and cede back to the states decisions about how and whether to evaluate teachers, and how to spend much of the money sent by Washington to educate poor, disabled and non-English speaking students. No Democrats supported the bill...Rep. John Kline (R-MN), the lead sponsor..."We should not tie thehands of teachers and school officials." This is the first change in a dozen years, that both Chambers of Congress has approved a comprehensive bill to update federal education law.

2013 Michael Doyle – McClatchy Newspapers

Farm Bill: Republicans in the House of Representatives on Thursday rammed through a revised farm bill *designed mostly to solve a vexing political problem that has divided their party* and frustrated farmers nationwide that includes crop subsidies and other farm benefits *but excludes nutrition programs including food* *stamps… **NOTE: Food stamp program left out of Farm Bill passed by House.***

September 20, 2013 – House cuts food stamp program 5%.

I noted this one in the paper and had to cut it out.

???Millions in US subsidies go to dead farmers; the Federal government pays millions of dollars in farm subsidies each year to farmers that have died, because *the Department of Agriculture lacks the proper controls to make sure the money it sends is going to the right people,* a government audit has found!!! So what happened to the money? Was it returned?

Also GOP to slash arts, environmental funding by 24 billion; included the Environmental Protection Agency by one-third, gutting that program, national endowments for the Arts by near one-half; the measure funding the Interior Department, EPA, national parks and federal firefighting is cut by 19% below funding in March!!! Slash and burn—slash and burn. That's the Budget Chairman's and the Speaker's way. **"We should not be judged how many new laws we create. Rather we should be judged on how many we repeal."**

STUDENT LOAN
www.usatoday.com/stort/news/nation/2014/08/25/student-loan
The Congressional Budget Office projects the government to clear $175 billion in profit over the next decade on student loans.

A law touted by politicians as their way of keeping money in the pockets of the nation's college students will instead funnel more than $700 million in additional profit into the federal government's wallet over the next 10 years… The law…was passed and signed by President Obama…as a win in the campaign to combat a rising tide of student loan indebtedness… Though the this will accomplish that in the short term… "As soon as the interest rates begin to go back up, this deal ends up worse for students and their parents… In total, the CBO projects the government to clear $175 billion in profit over the next decade on student loans. **2016** – This has been changed.

GENERAL STATISTICS

*In America the taint of secularism
is broad across the land. The nation
is sectarian rather than Christian.*

James Fenimore Cooper

James Fenimore Cooper's observation could not be more relevant than it is today. In this secular age of instant gratification we are heading down the road toward **moral bankruptcy.** The statistics show the deterioration that has set in. It is safe to say that people that have a life that is stable and balanced, live by strong moral and ethical values. I hope these people are still in the majority. The call for restraint in all areas of our lives is now being made. We are being drummed out by salacious advertising, and by some areas of the entertainment and unregulated TV industries that promote the latest type of delirious experience with complete abandon.

Our lives reflect the destruction. At the top, immorality in all of its forms, aided by drugs, alcohol, guns, and violence and sex, have taken over our homes, our streets and our nation. As a result, we have burdened ourselves and the country with the highest financial deficit in our history. As a nation, the cost of our medical issues and crime are at an all-time high including: obesity, mental health, high blood pressure, heart disease, cancer, diabetes and *social diseases;* adding skyrocketing costs to our already highest debt in history.

Our once most prosperous nation has an enormous amount of people who are homeless. While the number has declined, 610,042 were homeless with 215,344 living in "unsheltered areas." On July 28, 2013 CBS News reported that **80%** of adults are at or near poverty level. *Unemployment is stabilizing, but the loss of trillions of dollars in 2008, and the reported recovery of a mere $116 million as was recently reported, is not even a pittance of what has been lost.* Food banks cannot keep their shelves stocked as more and more of the population resort to this source of food to supplement their low incomes.

Paramount to our current state of affairs, **the stock market is at a new higher than high** which even has the most cautious of investors suggesting that we could fall into another major financial downturn; and all of this in a short seven years. There are some indications that a new monetary system will replace our currency with electronic money.   Electronic money is just that. Whole records are wiped out by a keystroke. There are signs that profit-taking is on the rise again. *And if it were to be put in place, anyone can be wiped out with one stroke.*

Through the years, since President Nixon took us off of the gold standard (August 15, 1973), Congress has seen fit to undue stringent safeguards in our monetary markets that were put in place during the time of the great Depression. The 1933 Glass/Steagall Act, now sponsored by Elizabeth W. Warren (D) - MA and John McCain (R) – AZ which *must be passed this upcoming session* as a beginning to provide a bulwark against another financial hemorrhage. **2016** – This area has been turned around,

Today's corporate leaders salary and benefit packages have gone into the millions of dollars, another new high, even in proportion to the great financial crash of 1929 and Depression, that lasted clear into the 1930's. Billionaires were unheard of before the 1980's. Millionaires are common today. Before Reagan's first term in office, a millionaire was held in awe and a million meant $1,000,000 in hard cash and equities, all tangibles, backed up by the gold standard.

Today we throw words such a trillions, $1,000,000,000,000 not just one, but our government owes ? trillion. And on up…who knows, the sky is the limit, or is it? This is electronic money. All of this since President Reagan's first term in office. All of this in a short 31 years, since this President dismantled programs that were designed to give support to those who had none.   During the Depression, one fourth – 25% of the population were out of work.
The following information is for the years: 1978 – 1988 from the book by: **KEVIN PHILLIPS, POLITICS OF RICH AND POOR – 1991**

Millionaires in the U.S. – 1978		450,000
Billionaires " 1978		1
Millionaires " 1988		1,500,000

Billionaires   "   1988   51

NOTE: Kevin Phillips is a Republican and the book came out during President Regan's terms in office. The book raised quite a storm after it was released.

2016 – Dramatic Jump in Millionaires

<u>www.nbc.com/business/economy/more</u>**... March 10, 2015**

There are 10.1 millionaires today...tops prerecession figure of 9.2 million in 2007.

<u>www.forbes.com</u> **– March 6, 2013**

There are 536 billionaires today and 6.15 millionaires which = 1 in 20 households, nationwide. Numbers don't include value of real estate.

In 25 years we have had an increase of – 391 billionaires
In 25 years we have had an increase of – 850,000 millionaires.

2016 –September, 2013 – <u>www.usa.com/story/momey/business/</u>
4 in 5 in USA face near-poverty, no work. Washington (AP)
Number of adult population estimated at 218 million in 2009; 5 years later it is safe to say at least 220 million plus. 4 out of 5 = 80%; 80% of 220 million = 176 million people fall into this category.

2016 – These figures have had a good change. The following information re: homeless are raw figures. It amazes me how they slice and dice these figures. Percentages are the terms of choice. I found it difficult to find a simple answer to simple question: How many people are homeless in the U.S. today?

What followed was detailed information that a person with a degree in *formula babble* to obtain information regarding how the formulation of how to correctly interpret the grafts and charts, has many approaches, depending on the material that is being presented and what the material that has been cited is being compared to with another set of criteria. I know all of you understand this. Now three figures that I am going to put down are:

- The median income in 2011 was $50,502, down 1.3% from 2010;
- The other figures re: the number of homeless in 2012 – 239,403 and 162,246 children, up 2.0 % over 2011.
- There are 261 millionaires in Congress; there are just plain millionaires, there are mega millionaires and mega, mega, millionaires.

http://documents.lahsa.org was the best site I was able to find. The title page showed that it was posted on **April 15, 2013.**

- The disparity between the two groups of figures clearly shows that the President's call for the top 5% certainly are able and should be paying more taxes.
- **The G. W. Bush tax credits need to be eliminated.**

It falls on all of us that value our way of life and trust the guarantees of the Constitution, to demand change. We need to reclaim our lives, and the lives of our children, as now with even more restraints in place. We need to reclaim our homes, streets, schools, businesses and our personal and national lives. This year, through the **voting booth** in November, we can start to clean out the nests of those in Congress that are advocating our ruin.

I have included a list of those in **Congress** who are bound to the lobbyist's/special interests, which includes the **NRA** and drug cartels that are making inroads into our heartland, the pornography industry and the insidious groups that are working for their governments to bring about the downfall of America.

We are seeing more and more unexplained major accidents and damage to our infrastructure. All of these areas just mentioned are the face of those in our society that are now trying to hold us hostage and destroying the fabric of our lives.

Through manipulation of many recent tragedies, they are preying on the fears of these events and stirring up people with rhetoric that

89

divides people and promotes an escalation of a downward spiral of confusion and mistrust in our legitimate police force to handle any crisis.

It has been suggested that we need armed guards in our schools. *As long as the children understand that the day will come when they are no longer needed, it is something that is necessary at this time.* But it is imperative that they also know why they are there. We have to assure them that this is a protective measure. The day will come when they will no longer be needed, but in the meantime they provide the security that is so necessary to growing children. *What the anarchists want is that the children are led to believe that this is the normal way of life and will always be this way. They come to accept being 'guarded by them'. It becomes a way of life.*

And when more and more of these guards are on the scene, they accept it as normal too. Children today will have a hard time learning what it means to be free and that life was not meant to be lived with somebody acting as guards all of the time. *These are the same tactics that were used in Europe during the 1930's before World War II.*

It is never too late to turn the tide. But we need to start today – we can't wait for tomorrow; tomorrow will be too late. Each of us needs to re-access our values and priorities for ourselves, our children and families, and our country. If we do not act now, we will go the way of all past great countries and empires. Our Light of Liberty will be put out.

We The People must be the agents for change to protect our most treasured and valued tenets of our heritage from our Founding Fathers. As the old adage goes: Stand for something or fall for anything.

THE VALUE OF
CONGRESSIONAL PERKS

NOTICE

ONLY THE VERY RICH
AND CONGRESSIONAL
PERSONEL ALLOWED

"therrress *"gold" in demm der walls*"

"They have kept us on a lean diet, so as good concerned stewards of our economy and the National Budget, we have an obligation to trim the fat from theirs." P.A. B.

PERKS: Until I checked this website, I don't ever remember any discussions being held about the perquisites (perks) enjoyed by Congress. One of the staples of every campaign is the vow to cut down on BIG GOVERNMENT AND GOVERNMENT WASTE. No wonder that we have Big Government; the cost of running both houses is staggering. The next section will take a look at the perks enjoyed by the members and their families for one year. I found information that suggested that the perks amount to a *staggering $4.5 billion a year (of your taxpayer money.)*

www.the-office.com/545/htm
Pay and Perquisites of Congress – Orlando Sentinel Columnist Charlie Reese

I will ask you to go to these websites; and read the full reports for complete information. If you have a printer, make a copy. This was written in 2011. I'll begin with the opening paragraph:

"One hundred senators, 435 congressmen, one President and nine Supreme Court justices equates to 545 human beings of the 300 million people in this country. It is those 545 people who are directly, legally, morally, and individually responsible for the domestic problems that plague this country."

"And speaking of holding these people accountable...*do you have ANY IDEA how much money, and how many special benefits you Congressman and your Senator have handed to them, at taxpayer expense every single year?*

"...next comes the mountain of perqs (pronounced "perks") that most Fortune 500 companies couldn't rival... But all members enjoy access to a separate piggy bank know as their "allowance." This funding generally goes toward maintaining their offices and building up a legislative entourage."

- Offices, furniture, and discount shopping privileges: $40,000 dollars and potentially more – for furniture in their home-state offices.

92

- They can deduct up to $3,000 for expenses while outside their home districts or states.
- **House:** Representatives up to $900,000 for salaries for up to 18 staff members. In 2009 maximum salary for a staffer in a member's personal office-$168,411.
- **Senate:** …same privilege but much *bigger* allowance for Office expenses… the average allocation for fiscal 2010 was more than $3.3 million.
- **Senators** may higher between 26 and 60 aides… but for starters for three legal assistants.
- Up to $75, 000 can be transferred from staff funds into his or there official expense account Expense Allowances for members, kept separate from personal staff allowances, cover domestic travel, and expenses related to running the offices(s).
- Free postage for letters and packages.
- Free Domestic Travel (to and from District/State).
- Free foreign travel to conduct government business finances through special allowances. These funds can come from various sources.
- Workdays – average three-and one-half if you count Monday nights.

http://wwww.the-office.com/545htm

To finish off this debacle, I was amazed to see the following article by **Lynn Hulsey** – *Cox Newpapers* printed in our paper, The Olympian, on Sunday, February 17, 2013.

Here are some of her highlights: The article starts out with the following caption: "Even haircuts for Senate costing taxpayers."

"…Since 1997 the Senate Hair Care shop has consistently run deficits of about $340,000 annually. (For 15 years this amounts to $5.1 million dollars – our taxpayer money). Last year the deficit was $401,000 (2012)." This again is a lengthy article, if you go online to The Olympian, I am sure you will be able to access the full in-depth article. Three items she points out are as follows:

- …generous pension that allows a member to retire at 62 with a full pension after (just) five years of civilian federal service.
- Rides on a private subway system that runs between offices, committee rooms and the Capital.
- Up to $.96 per mile for mileage reimbursement.

While Congress members pay for their haircuts ($20.00), other services such as photography and recording studios are covered by their office allowance ($75,000 a year for office, as per the Pay and Perks report—taxpayer money—are provided free of charge.)

- The lead Senate photographer makes $100,000 a year—the median income for photographers in Washington, D.C. in 2011 was $65,332.
- The Senate cabinet shop…frames photographs, hand-built chairs and cabinets… The shop supervisor earned $107,484… (What happens to the "old" furniture?)
- The Senate *hair salon* provides about 509 services a week including, shampooing, coloring and waves, nail services, *hair removal*, (italics mine)… One stylist earned $79,202 annually, another $74,615 (as they say in Vegas—does that include 'tokes'?)
- It costs about $900,000 a year to operate. By comparison, a hair stylist in Washington, D.C. $40,934; a barber $49,920. The guy who gives shoe shines at $6.00 per hour, earned $40,432.

Take a member from one of the largest states and apply these numbers to one person. *You can see why the estimated perks are said to be as much as $4.5 billion a year.*

And this, my friends is how hard it is to be a member of the Congressional body of 545 members.

Did you read the above mentioned two reports—are you enthralled **or _galled?!!!_**

THE VALUE OF REVIEW OF
RECENT HISTORY AND
POSSIBLE TRENDS

"History teaches perhaps few clear lessons.
But surely in such lessons learned by the world
at great cost, is that aggression unopposed
becomes a contagious disease."

President Jimmy Carter
39th President of the United States

AN ASSESSMENT

The current picture appears to be a world in crisis and that we are in "the third world war". Some people have already alluded to this same possibility. It is a war of "competition aided by electronics and cyber theft," plus extreme idealists and people that have no other intention but to tear down our Constitution and Bill of Rights and all governments who champion their people.

The credit card came into public use in the early 70's. Although not recognized at the time, this was the signal of the right-wingers in the highest reaches of government to ramp up the steady inroads they had made beginning during the Eisenhower administration, to systematically take our government apart.

Only once, since President Reagan's term to the present, were we current fiscally; when President Clinton left office. Reagan's time in office was the beginning of massive use of electronic money by catering to the growing right wing element in our political system, now the right wing ultra-neo-conservatism. The Tea Party has elected themselves the designated party to become the standard bearer.

When The Lid Opened On Pandora's Box

All governments engage in finding weak spots is competing governments. This is as old as time. However, technology, having progressed to the current level, has opened new and faster methods of gaining information.

NSA/Cyber Warfare: As we are all too clear with the latest leaks of national security information, we are now hearing very loud and *vociferous howls to curtail "spying."* It does appear that the recent events *may* have been mishandled, *but,* policies are going to have to be developed to protect ourselves from the now ongoing, worldwide spying. *We are now engaged in warfare-cyber warfare. It will not cease until we come to terms with every person on this planet, not just governments.* We are in for another very long haul.

We are going to have to bite the bullet and realize that our country must have the capability to defend ourselves in this new cyber climate. Why can any government (most recently China) steal our information without some kind of penalty? *Who inside our Hallowed Halls,* are aiding and abetting the worldwide network?

Communism: While China and Russia have a softer image, their message is still the same. In 1956 Nikita Khrushchev, Soviet Premier, said: "We will bury you." "Whether you like it or not, history in on our side; we will win you in." 8/9/1960 GT/GS. It is not my intention to quibble with this exact translation 'dig you in'; the intent has been from the early in 1900's, when Communism made its start to control the world.

Along with Communism, in a very short 60 years, we are also the main target of those who were beaten when Hitler's Nazi Regime was crushed. President Truman and Prime Minister Winston Churchill, both felt very strongly the Stalin was not going to agree to amenable terms in the settlement of Europe, when the Yalta Agreement in 1945, ending World War II.

Communism received a major setback when the Berlin Wall came down; but since then they have just retrenched. They are as interested as ever in seeing the western world fall. China and Russia represent eastern and western thought; which vision of Communism will prevail, remains to be seen. I think it is more of a style of leadership. The principle is the same.

Our democratic form of government has grown. It all goes back to our unique Constitution and Bill of Rights; as written, they are singular. New democracies that are springing up all over the world have used our system as a starting point for developing their constitutions, but have adapted elements that better fit their populations and way of life.

Types of Government - For people that do not have a complete grasp of our government, I am including the following.

The two government systems that have withstood the test of time are the *English Constitutional Monarchy established in 1689.* The English do not have a written Constitution. And Democracy as defined by our American Constitution and Bill of Rights was signed in 1776; well over 240 hundred years ago.

The English Constitutional Monarchy – 1689 was the year that the Crown relinquished rule of the empire with the passage of the English Bill of Rights. The Crown gave up their rule and agreed to terms that..."the Constitutional Monarchy and PARLIAMENT were to rule England together."

Fascism: An authoritarian and right-wing system of government and social organization. In Nazi Germany during World Would II. Adolph Hitler adopted this fascist form of government. The dictator Benito Mussolini was ruler of Italy, during this period of history. Italy had been under Fascism rule 1925. Mussolini joined Hitler in the later thirties.

The Iroquois Nation, comprised of Six Indian Nations in the upper-northeast area had a participatory form of government since the 1100's. It is interesting that this form of ruling the people was here in our native population before the migration from Europe. So on our soil, besides having the oldest, working written constitution a type of democracy had been in effect in that part of the country for 500 years prior to the migration starting in the 1400's. It has held our country in good stead.

And now with the ongoing, urgent issues that we are facing today, we have to have faith in the knowledge that our system is still as viable, as when it was completely finalized in the late 1780's. We will find the answers to our challenges, **if** we have a Congress that will work together to keep our Constitution intact.

Another threat that is now always possible is by aiding and abetting our enemies attaining our TOP SECRET information. And today, a marauding element is spreading everywhere on the planet. The whole world is suffering from their manipulations through our individual economies by pirating credit card and personal information.

Since the 1980's **Islam** has now come to the front. It is clear in my mind they are fomenting their seeds of dominance there too, with the end in mind of getting full control of that part of the world and spreading with more and more militant groups coming up. This is not what all of the Muslim world wants or is about. The population from the Muslim world is growing here in our country; and reports of hate crimes against these people are growing.

We have to remember that there are two factions in Islam; the Sunni's and Shia's. Just reading on the web the majority of those professing Islam are the Sunni's. Go to the website on Islam and you will quickly get a grasp of what is going on in that part of the world. By reading about Saddam Hussein and what led up to the war in Iraq, world affairs come more into focus. Another note, Al Qaeda is primarily Sunni, who almost from the beginning have been fighting each other to for dominance in their religion. Right now the Sunni's seem to have the upper hand. This too, is part of their history.

The latest tragedy is Syria's use of nerve gas on 1,400 plus people with as many as 400 children killed in the process. This is a game changer. A new line has been drawn. Time has passed and these weapons are being removed, but who knows when they will surface again.

www.u-s-history.com/pages/h1740.html.
The Muslim religion was formed in the 7th century. Divisions among them became apparent very early on caused by a split in the leadership that resulted with the two main contenders, the Shia's and Sunni's. This protracted war we have been involved in will be ongoing, because some portion of these people believe that they should fight to death for their faith.

~

www.faithfacts.org/world-religions Similarities between
Judaism, Christianity and Islam

Judaism, Christianity, and Muslim faiths have some beliefs in
common. We all believe that we are descendants of Abraham. We
all agree that there is one God who created the universe and is
sovereign in the lives of men. We agree that God is the source of
justice and morality. We agree that His ultimate justice is
dispensed via life after death in heaven and hell. We consider such
things as pornography and licentious living as pollutants to society.
In fact, one of the reasons for the strong negative reaction to
western civilization in Muslim countries is the influence of such
practices emanating from the west.

But there are many things upon which we disagree. The points of
disagreement touch on every important religious doctrine...

There are Muslims who are gracious and peace-loving people. As I
understand from a small amount of reading, Islam has elements of
peacefulness in it. However, anyone who wants to commit violence
has perfect justification for doing so from the Quran. The initial call
was for death to all non-believers of Islam. Violence and death is
part of Muslim doctrine.

I cannot urge you strongly enough to read this full discussion. In
the few short pages, the language is clear and concise; by grasping
this amount of information, we will better understand our new
neighbors and hopefully be able to engage in meaningful dialogue
for education on both sides.

Exchange of ideas is the best way to clear future misunderstandings.
Some people who believe in Islam' have chosen to become citizens
of our country and have been given the opportunity to move among
us. For further growth and diversity in our country, we must extend
our hands in friendship. *This is what makes our country strong and
a land free of repression.* This is the way we can continue to keep
the light of freedom shining. The crisis we are facing today is which
current political philosophy will prevail.

- **Anarchists/Rogues**: Aspire to world rule by massive manipulation of the world political and monetary systems; permeating all governments through channels they build into every governmental system; their aim is total control through all currencies in the world.
- **Democracy:** respect for all people, and the right of each people, to have a voice in how we are going to live; maintaining our own identity as a people, and living in harmony, collectively.
- **Communism:** the state, having full control, determines all the rules and regulations of its people. Their stronghold in Asia in the east and Russia in the west, control a large part of the physical world.

Islam: Based on the Koran, is a dual way of life. Their religious convictions and type of government is all- encompassing in all facets of their lives. From the beginning of Islam, in the mid-seventh century, has rejected the principles of Judaism and Christianity. They believe that Mohammed was asked by God the Father to lead people to follow the word of the Koran, and to fight to the death (non-believers) infidels. Mohammed is the Profit of this new religion, replacing Moses and the Laws governing Judaism and Christianity.

Judaism: Follows the laws based in the Torah in how they live their lives and believe in the hereafter.

Christianity: The chief difference between Judaism and Christianity is in regard to the Messiah. Judaism believes that Jesus Christ was a prophet. Christians believe that Jesus Christ is the Son of God.

Mormon: There is one more facet to these three religions, the Mormon faith. Joseph Smith stablished the Mormon Church in 1830, The Church of Christ of the Latter Day Saints after having vision when he was younger. Their creed is called the Book of Mormon. Through their ministry, young men go on a mission for one year to spread the word. Joseph Smith is thought as the latest profit to carry the word of God. Rejecting all Christian religions, the Book of Mormon is word they preach and live by. They use the Christian bible as a background for their beliefs, *but it is not Christian*. It is a fast growing religion.

So we must call all good people around to world to settle your differences with those that you don't agree. The Bible tells us that God said "My House has many mansions." We want the same good things in life that all achieve through compromise. We must work together to find a middle ground that all will recognize and is equitable to the majority of people. We have arrived at this point in history: it will boil down to good vs. evil, worldwide.

History shows that the Monarchy Parliamentary and American Democratic systems have had the most success, starting in England in 1689. In both systems, we have had our share of extreme differences. The key to our success is our form of government, where all people have a voice through two governing bodies, Parliament and Congress; by talking and compromising to come to consensus for all of our citizens.

As a result we are a viable, robust people, connected in our faith in each other, individually and collectively. I believe the world knows we are a vocal people and do not hesitate to stand up for our beliefs. The fact that I can write this book is proof, that every individual has a voice. The strength of our system is that we can put our beliefs out and the public forum will say yea or nay.

Our cherished values include: Freedom of Speech; Freedom of Religion: Freedom of Assembly: Freedom from fear of retaliation from our government for voicing our views. We change our leaders and our laws through the ballot box. No one that has enjoyed these guarantees as our birthright is going to let anyone deprive us of our way of life.

We have shown that we have weathered all storms and armed with this strength of the people and by the people we will continue to meet our destiny until the *clarion call is sounded*

Science has proven that no accurate estimate can be given for how long the world has existed. In our Western world, our history is divided by epochal changes.

https://sites.google.com/a/fwparker.org/ - They are as follows:

EPOCH One: The Epoch of Origins (5,000 BCE-500   BCE)
- EPOCH Two: The Epoch of Advancement (500 BCE-1492 CE)
- EPOCH Three: The Epoch of Interactions (1400-1920)
- EPOCH Four: The Epoch of Conflict (1920-1990)
- Conclusion: A History driven by Interaction.

I thought it curious that the current epoch was referred to as "Conclusion." I don't think along these lines, but everything I have written is just my point of view, from my very sparse formal education. I don't pretend to any professionalism in what I have written.

The fourth epoch, lasting only 70 years, is an indication though that the current state of the world will not take that many years to come to a conclusion. The period that we are in, at this very early time in this epoch, is the connectivity of the whole world through all types of electronic communication. How we proceed into the future will be determined by what ideology prevails.

"We will see Armageddon or the Third Millennium", author Thomas Merton wrote, as other voices have been saying the same thing. I do not believe that the end of the world is eminent. However, I do feel that if we cannot turn our current challenges, we will see the end of democracy as we know it today. (It ceased being a true Democracy when Capitalism took over completely in the mid-70's.) As noted above our government very easily could become and oligarchy, that usually leads to a dictatorship. This is what our enemies are in the process of doing. "We will bury you..." from communist Russia... Fascism and... jihad are all vying to break our democracy today. The clock is ticking.

"Give me liberty or give me death…" are the famous words of Patrick Henry, from Virginia in the days of the Revolution. He served as Governor for one year as the first post-Colonial Governor. He was a representative to the first Continental Congress, but didn't attend the second. He died in 1796. His statement is a call to us today if we do not tyranny to replace our lives today.

~

"God grants liberty only to those who love it…"
Daniel Webster in 1830

~

Every act of aggression that has been committed started with the first thought and feeling of being transgressed against; from the smallest incident to the most horrendous of genocides and war. From the beginning of time to now, it is impossible to put a number on the number of people killed. Wars are futile, because you cannot kill thought and the resultant feelings that come with these thoughts, good or bad.

All evidence points to the fact that we are now in the period of confronting good over evil. September 11, 2014 was the thirteenth anniversary of the destruction of the Twin Towers and parts of the Pentagon. The ensuing years have brought us to this point in our history for resolution to the ever widening divides that have gained monumental volume, like a wave swelling to crest during these past 13 years.

How we resolve these new coming challenges will be determined by what we can accomplish in the way of forcing out the rogue forces that are poised to take full control of our country and deal with them through our courts.

As the longest lasting Democracy, this time for us is critical. If we are not successful, we will not be able and ready to face the ultimate showdown with the rest of the world when that ultimate challenge arrives. We must be successful as the results will determine the direction we will take as we move forward into this new 3rd millennium. We must begin with the upcoming election to start change in Congress.

A bipartisan commission needs to be formed to start the investigation that will focus on those outside Congress; starting with former cabinet officials, the NRA, banking and the source of the money supply that has provided the backing for all activities that have widened the inroads into dismantling our Democratic government and way of life.

And to the enemies within: We in America are committed to democracy. We have and will continue to aid those that are striving for self-government. The battle is joined. This battle for hearts and souls of mankind will not be the end of the world; only the world as we know it today. When the base of any structure grows larger than the top, the top crumbles. This is our challenge today. *We will not lose.* This book is my attempt to help broaden the base, so that every American's voice will be heard. *Take this to heart.*

Suggested Readings:

I think the following are seminal books. Earlier, I referred to the book published in 1990 – **The Politics of Rich and Poor by Kevin Phillips.** It is the best book of the history of President Reagan's time in office and the beginning of where we are today. **Note:** Kevin Phillips is a registered Republican.

It is as pertinent today as when it was released. Its message travels right up to today. On the cover of the book is the following commentary: "Incisive…A devastating critique that has already fueled furious pros and cons in Washington" – USA Today.

In 1991, **Albert Hourani's book: A History of the Arab Peoples,** was published; Ira M. Lapidus, University of California Berkley comments, "…broad in its coverage of the whole Arab world and the Arab era in the Middle Eastern history for pre-Islamic Arabia to contemporary times."

Mr. Hourani deals with a full range of issues – empires and states, the structures of societies and elites, religion, including demographic movements. ... "Difficult issues ranging from political policies to the Palestinian question to the role of women in society…are treated with even-handed, balanced and detached judgment." He wrote extensively about Islam and was a noted teacher and lecturer. His story will be of interest to those who have a strong interest in the mid-East.

From Mein Kampf

"I shall give propagandists cause for starting the war. Never mind, whether it is plausible or not. The victor will not be asked, later on, whether he told the truth or not. In starting and waging a war, it is not Right that matters but Victory."

"Have no pity. Adopt a brutal attitude…Right is on the side of the strongest." Adolph Hitler - Speech to high officers August 22, 1939." This one of the quotes **George Seldes** included in his book **The Great Thoughts.**

George Santayana. "It is by reading and learning of the past that we gain the knowledge to help direct our efforts in challenges that face us today. "Those who do not know the past are bound to repeat it (mistakes)."

Adolph Hitler's Mein Kampf, meaning "My Struggle" is his roadmap to conquer the world. History certainly shows his struggle to create a new society, by murdering over six million Jews and other races too that did not make the grade of what he had in mind: a pure Aryan race. This book is like a bible, to people that have embraced his message. *The pattern of the Tea Party has many of the elements of fascism.*

Some question the relevance of Hitler's book to our political structure today. However, it does show what happens when people in high places develop too narrow of a focus, as we have seen over the last 60 years. It shows the lengths they will go to achieve their ends. All of the uprisings to gain democracy since World War II are a testament to the clash of ideals.

William Shirer wrote what many consider the best history of this era in his book: **The Rise and Fall of the Third Reich.** History buffs of this time frame know of this work. It is fascinating reading.

Through compiling this book, I have learned that:

"Any Government is only as stable as its laws are sound, and the structure as strong as its base."

Our laws have been eroding very rapidly with the pardon of President Richard Nixon after he was impeached. Mentally this set the tone for the country, that no crime is too large or scope too broad for those that have the will to exercise it. Since Reagan's terms in office we can see the boldness of those in high places resulting in the 2008 meltdown.

2016 - NOTE: It was 32 years ago September 8, 1974 that President Gerald Ford pardoned Richard Nixon. I feel this was a grave error on judgment.

ALEX – The American Legal Counsel, was founded by the Koch Brothers Industries began in 1973. It became the legal arm of Koch Industries. They conducted secret meetings form 1973 to the present. Their set purpose was to change the structure of our government. They accomplished this by people in this organization who had succeeded in gaining seats in Congress.

David Koch had run for Vice President in 1980 on the Libertarian Party ticket. He had many friends and people, who were willing to help them achieve their goals. He established a "grass roots"* cadre, in the Republican Party. They were able to have new laws implemented in all levels of government, national, state, county and city. They removed safeguards that kept law and order, and control that protected of our Democratic values.

The structure of our social order was accomplished by removing moral and ethical standards of living for all; cut programs for the lower class, poor and indigents. They cut funding through key legislation that removed laws and safe guards, which were in place to protect society from unscrupulous and criminal acts, and cut valuable funding to keep our schools as first place among nations.

The following show how well they have accomplished their goals:**

2016 - www.rankingamerica.wordpress/catagory/education

This is another complete report of America rankings world-wide:

Rank: 14th in education
24th in literacy
17th in education performance
 6th in reading
12th in first sex education
23rd in PISA science
54th in education expenditures…
14th in foreign students, studying education…
95th in private high school students…
34th in student living scale…
134th for government aid to education

www.npr.org/section/the-two_way/2013**: standings in math, reading and science.*****

American 15 year olds continue to turn in flat results in a test that measures students' proficient in reading, math, and science world-wide *failing to crack the global top 20.*
2016 – Note: *** Please read all of the above reports. Also see page 137 for further notes on edcation

Note: this in depth report of the Koch empire, details the 80 year history of... at:
www.rollingstone.com/political/...koch-brothers-toxic-empire

Note: All of these noted websites <u>must be read</u> *to get the full grasp of where we are currently.*

Now the question is: What direction will the country go...?

MAN'S INHUMANITY TO MAN

AND THE HEAVENS
CRY OUT FOR JUSTICE
...AND FOR MERCY

"Under the rule of the
"Dollar" Human life has
fallen to its lowest value."

Charles A. Lindbergh Sr.

Don't wait for the last judgment,
It takes place every day."

Albert Camus

2016 – Too much has happened since 2013, I just can't add any more, nor do I want to go over all of the tragedies since then.

By: United Nations - Andrew MacCaskill and Karitkay Mehrotra – Bloomberg News – New Delhi

RAPE: Brutal rapes in India have been getting worldwide attention. The heinous rape and murder of a young women medical student over a year ago resulted in the perpetrators being hung for this crime. Since then, there have been more, with the latest being of "a 12 year girl abducted at gunpoint, then raped and murdered.

When the father found out that night he went to the police station "and said the two officers on duty, mocked him, ripped up his complaint and told him to come back in the morning. The father persisted begging them to act... the next day two girls (a 14year old niece of the family) were founding hanging from a tree in 115 degree heat...three cousins that lived close by, were arrested for kidnapping, rape and murder... the two policemen were fired and arrested on grounds of dereliction of duty and conspiring with the accused. An autopsy confirmed that the girls had been gang raped and after they were raped and hung from a tree."

"In spite of massive street demonstrations in the past two years protesting sexual assault and the passage of a tough new anti-rape law, incidents of rapes do not appear to have declined."

No mention of a trial and sentencing has taken place as yet.
Another story from the **Washington Post** in New Delhi, " that "a 19 year-year old woman was found hanging from a tree after allegedly being raped... The cause of death was not immediately confirmed. Police said there were no obvious signs of murder and that the woman might have committed suicide."

http://news.msn.com/world/one-in-10-girls-sexually-abused-worldwide. **Around 120 million girls around the world, close to one in 10, have been raped or sexually assaulted by the time**

111

they turn 10, a new UN report has found.   (See further stats on pornography on pg.150)

Kidnappings

The world is still shuddering at the kidnapping of 220 girls by Boko Haran, a jihadist militant group on April 16, 2014 (20 escaped.) Then another report of 91 people kidnapped including toddlers the youngest just 3 years old, 60 girls and women, some who were married, and 31 boys included. **2016 -** So much has happened, we have lost track on this story, but there have been continuing stories of the BoKo Haran's continuing with their kidnappings.

POVERTY AND HUNGER – Bread for The World.com
1.2 billion live in dire poverty in the world today and 842 million are still are hungry in the world today. This report said that 2.6 million children die every year from hunger.

How is it possible for anyone to take a look at the whole wide spectrum of the "haves and have not's" and not have some twinge of conscience, that we are not doing more for our brothers and sisters to relieve some of the misery that exists. The world depends on us for help and we can't even help our own, thanks to the $12.8 trillion for the Iraq/Afghanistan by the current and recent leaders in Congress.

NOTE: While in the Philippines a number of years ago, we were out at 10 ten o'clock at night, and stopped for a red light. Little children, three, four and five year olds, bare foot, in grubby clothes, matted hair, dirty faces, unwashed and rubbing their little hands on the windows of the car, crying, peso, peso, peso. And all a person can do is to move along in the traffic with the lingering sound of peso, peso, peso, hanging in the air.

No one can talk on this subject and not give a HEARTFELT THANK YOU to all that are giving *their all* to help. We here in the United States are a very generous people. So the question to me is how can we have this same scenario and this kind of activity be taking place here, in the richest country in the world? And WHY should any child in the world have to live like this? *This is the worldwide QUESTION AND STORY.*

I have chosen to include this segment in this part of the book because the time was during World War II. There are threads from that time to what is happening now, even though in and of themselves the stories may not draw a clear distinction. But they do show what happens when world affairs spin out of control and rogue elements are at the head of governments.

The people that perpetrated these crimes have descendants that are alive today, and the evil that existed then is more virulent than ever. It has permeated the whole world with the multiple genocides that have taken place since this war, and crimes that we have never heard of.

It is very clear to me that we are being taken over by insidious interests that have made inroads to slowly destroy our way life. They are eroding our treasured liberties, foam distrust and have hamstrung our top agencies through many other means. As a result, our lives have deteriorated to new low levels.

Few Americans under the age of 75 remember what it is like to be under real war conditions. It is not possible for our native born to understand what it means to be under war time regulations for your own safety and the safety of the whole country. Our very large immigrant population understands more than those who are American born.

The majority of immigrants came to our shores to escape unacceptable conditions in their former homeland. They have had firsthand experience in dealing with the unbearable strife and threat to their lives in far too many cases. The influx now is from all over globe.

In earlier times, these people came mostly from Europe. The new major exodus started as a result of World War II. We know their stories from first hand verbal histories and through pictures that have so graphically depicted the horrors they had to endure. Fortunately their stories have spread around the globe.

I am most familiar with European history and have never focused on the war progression of events in Asia. During World II, my oldest brother served in both the European and Pacific wars. A cousin of mine was in the war in the Pacific. He was captured and imprisoned by the Japanese, early in the war.. I was only eight years old when World War II started. When this cousin came home after the war and he had been released, he never recovered fully from being captured. He wasn't even able to socialize with his own family.

His mother told my Mom that he would only eat off of a metal pan, placed in a corner. He crouched over his food facing the wall. After we had moved to California, from Denver, Colorado, a war veteran friend of the family came to visit and brought with him his friend, a man that had survived the Bataan Death March.

A recent story in our newspaper told of another survivor of the Bataan Death March here in our state, who had all of his medals from this war (a picture showed how many medals he had received) stolen including the medal he had received as a survivor of the Death March.

Since the end of World War II, the overriding worry was the spread of Communism. The stories of the chilling events in Cambodia, and Laos and elsewhere in Asia during the Viet-Nam war never made the headline news in the way that the Holocaust did in Western Europe. We didn't have the technology that we have today. The news of the war in Viet-Nam and the backlash that followed in its wake was the overriding news and well, *it was the sixties...*

World War II, the Korean War, and the Viet-Nam war were "over there." For me the advent of these books from someone like a medical doctor Dr. Tom Dooley, brought home that Asia was not *really that far away.* On a globe of the world, you really have to look to see where they are located.

Dr. Tom Dooley joined the Navy after receiving his medical degree. With his years in the Navy and those following, he worked a total of 14 years. After his service in the Navy, he resigned and stayed to continue working with the refugees from Viet-Nam and Taiwan, who were relocated to Saipan and continued working in Cambodia and Laos. The web catalog of works about Dr. Dooley is 129 pages in length.

The three individual books were combined and sold under the title: The Three Great Books by Dr. Tom Dooley. I read the three books that Dr. Dooley wrote of his experiences for 14 years, before he died from melanoma cancer, at the age of 34.

The original song Tom Dooley is from North Carolina about a murderer, Thomas C. Dula (pronounced (Dooley). Who was hung, in the 1866. The Kingston Trio sang the song in memory of Dr. Tom Dooley.

The first book was called: Deliver Us From Evil; the second: The Edge Of Tomorrow and the final book: The Night They Burned The Mountain. I cannot write of the horrors that were inflicted on these innocent victims, *especially the children.*

I can hardly write this much; they every bit equal what the victims of the Holocaust endured and in some cases were worse, because these children, left as deaf mutes had to live out their lives, not being able to speak or hear because of the ways they lost these abilities because of how they were tortured.

All of the books detail unimaginable suffering, as a result of the brutality of the Communists. As hard as these books are to read, the stories are riveting. The number of people that were murdered and maimed, by the Khmer Rouge and Pol Pot, their leader, final count was 3,314,768 from 1975 – 1979.

www.worldgenocide,org/conflicts. **Please read**.
Many men were held captive for multiple years in the prisons in Asia, as well as, in Europe; we don't know their stories, we do know of Republican Senator from Arizona, John McCain who was held in captivity in the "Hanoi Hilton" for five years, also known as "the hole." Their war records are a testament of their resiliency and a reflection of bravery and valor of those in the heat of battle.

To really understand the precariousness of the world today, read about the history from the 1930's just through World II, about what went on in Asia, and read too about Rwanda and much of Africa, and the various regimes in the 60's and 70's. **1990** – the Rwanda genocide killed 800,000 in just 100 days, the shortest and largest on record.

www.huffingtonpost.com//2013/12/06 Read **Nelson Mandela's** story and why he spent 27 years in prison for ending apartheid. Read the European history during the Nazi years. Read about the uprising of Poland after World War II. Read the story of India's struggle, to be free of rule from England, led by the revered Mahatma Gandhi. Peaceful resistance was the recourse given to them, as they couldn't compete on the battlefield with England. The movie "Gandhi" tells the story of the people that chose to die to earn the freedom from colonial rule.

Read of the destruction of almost all Europe and England, during this Great War that started with Hitler's domino effect, of one country falling after another, until Winston Churchill was appointed Prime Minister by England to take charge of the war. Read about our "Lend Lease" program, devised by our President and the Prime Minister of England and how the President got around Congress (who was denying what was happening in Europe) to give aid to England starting in 1939.

General George C. Marshall was Chief of Staff from 1939-1945 in Europe during World War II and then was Secretary of State in President Truman's Cabinet from 1947-1949. He was the author of the Marshal Plan that put Europe back together after the war.

116

AUSCHWITZ SURVIVORS Mr and Mrs Fels: In 1972 my husband was hospitalized for major surgery. When admitted he was put in a four bed ward. All four men were in for serious cases of cancer. Mr. Fels was across the room on the other side. We did not meet at the time before their surgeries. The man next to my husband was a professional singer born in Hawaii and died from his cancer. He had terminal cancer of the mouth and throat. The man directly across of the room was in for a cancerous brain tumor. He was 37 years old. I don't know if he survived.

Three months later, my husband had to go in for his three month checkup. When I got to the waiting room that day, very few seats were available, not unusual. There was a seat in the middle of a packed row and I took it. As I sat down I saw the right arm of the woman in the next chair with a number tattooed on her wrist. We nodded to each other. She said that she recognized me from when I visited my husband before his surgery and then told me that her husband was in that ward too.

That was how we met, in the family waiting room at the UCLA Medical Center. Mr. and Mrs. Fels were both survivors of the Death Camps and were in Auschwitz when General Patton freed them after the war was over. They were taken to a holding area of apartments that had been provided for the refugees. They both had rooms in this building and this is how they became acquainted.

Mrs. Fels and I had time to talk while we were both waiting for our husbands after their checkups. As we talked, she told me about her husband when he was first picked up by the Nazi's, was beaten and tortured; his medical problems stemmed for that time. She went on to tell me her story. She, her first husband, their two year old son, and her mother-in-law were all picked up together. When they got to Auschwitz her husband and son were put into one line and she and her mother-in-law were put in another. That was the last time she saw them.

This group of 200 women were put into a large single room that barely held all of them. They were stripped of all their clothing and

117

left completely naked. The never were given any clothes. There was an enclosed compound with very high walls. The women were all turned out in to this area everyday regardless of the weather, in all seasons; sun rain, sleet and snow, for 12 hours a day. I don't know how long she was there; I didn't think to ask her. Guards with guns walked on top of the wall guarding them for the full amount of time. As the women began to die their bodies were stacked along one wall. Their numbers grew daily.

In the building the windows were very high. The only way anyone could look out was to stand on someone else's shoulders. Mrs. Fels and her mother-in-law took turns. It was her mother-in-law's turn to look out of the window. When she came down, she was in a daze; she has seen her son and grandson walk into the gas chamber.

Mrs. Fels knew what she had seen, as so many others already had. Mrs. Fels told me that if she had seen what was happening she would have found a way to be with them, that way they would have all been together.

Time went by and Mrs. Fels mother-in-law's body was thrown on the stack, along with the others. When she was taken out of that compound and put into another prison, 170 bodies were stacked against the wall.

When she was finally released, her weight had dropped to half of what she had weighed when they were picked up. She described herself as looking like a skeleton. She was one of the prisoners to be freed by General Patton's soldiers.

Way To Freedom: The only way they could be released from the compound, was by writing their names on a slip of paper and throwing them out the window to the sidewalk many floors below. They watched as the little pieces slowly fluttered to the ground. These slips of paper didn't always make it to their intended destination. The wind would blow them away, or they missed their mark. The pe ople in the town were diligent in picking up these pieces of paper; they knew of the refugees housed there. Walking by, they would pick up these pieces of paper and took full responsibility for the refugee as named on these slips of paper. Of course the refugees had nothing except what had been given to them at the time of their release, clean clothes, housing with running water and able to take a shower or bath. They were now safe and secure.

These generous people accepted full responsibility; every expense that was incurred for their refugee dependents came out of their own purse. The object of course, was to get these refugees settled. Besides the released prisoner refugees, Europe was swarming with all of displaced people in bombed out Europe. At times this mission of love became overwhelming, because of the influx of people from all over Europe who had been displaced by the war. Making the arrangements and obtaining the required documentation needed by the country that would accept them included a great deal of red tape.

And this was the process these survivors had to go through to get back into the real world again. There were so many of them, some countries set quotas of the amount of these refugees they would accept. Mr. and Mrs. Fels, (I never knew her former name; they married shortly after they were rescued). Their wait lasted three months before their slip was picked up and finally, FREEDOM.

She opened her purse and brought out her wallet and showed me a picture of her son, a beautiful two year old tow headed boy; a big smile covering his face. She didn't tell me how she was able to recover this picture. And I never asked how many years she was in prison. I know that it must have been most of the war.

Another story from this time was about Father Maximillian Kolbe, a Catholic Priest. A prisoner had escaped from one of the blocks holding the prisoners. A group had been assembled to die by starvation. The gestapo (SS – secret police) called out a man to be the next victim to take the place of the escapee. He broke down crying "My wife, "My children." Father Kolbe stepped in and said that he would take his place.

Then the group was asked who would take his place and Father Kolbe stepped forward. He was tied up and led away to where he would die. They came to a door and that was opened to stairs leading down into a very deep chamber with no lights. Stilled tied up, he was pushed down these stairs. There were nine more in the room. They were never seen or heard from again. They were there to die. After 10 days, if no one died, the gestapo came down into the room and all those that were still alive, were given a lethal injection. These men were cleared out and the process started all over again. Somehow, the young man was saved and lived through the war. He later told of his story and that of Father Maximillian Kolbe. The main source for information can be found at: www.ushman.org/en/articles.

Edith Stein too, was sent to the gas chambers in August, 1942. She was the first woman of Jewish birth and faith to be baptized into the Catholic Church. Edith was a philosopher and was a leader in women place in the world. Edith's story has been the source of many books and articles. I encourage you to read the life of her truly dedicated life.

PARTT THREE

AND THE VALUE OF FAMILY LIFE?

He mocks the people who proposes that the
they in
In turn will care for the laboring poor.

(Stephen) Grover Cleveland
22nd and 24th President of
The United States

TRAGIC FAMILY STATISTICS

*There must be something radically
wrong with a system (capitalism)
that give rise to such social injustice.*

Pope Paul VI

FAMILY LIFE*:* This section of statistics shows how the quality of our lives has deteriorated. This is the other side of the coin to the **"GOOD LIFE."**

LEGALIZE THE HISPANIC POPULATION - IMMIGRATES
At the forefront of current issues, are those whose lives are entwined with ours through their long years of labor in the fields harvesting our crops now the food on our tables. While living here they lived by our rules and paid taxes. This migrant population was brought here because it was a ready pool of labor. Their hardships were many and the wages low. They deserve to become eligible for citizenshp. As the process has been outlined, they will go through the same process of all those eligible to become citizens.

Today, the Hispanic population in our country is facing these same challenges to become citizens of the United States. Our whole history shows that newcomers to our shores have had to earn recognition. **Cesar Chavez,** born outside of Yuma, Arizona in 1927, learned early what it meant to be Hispanic and disenfranchised.

His father had an accident that prevented him from working, which meant that his mother would have to work, so Cesar dropped out of high school and took her place to work in the fields of California. Working with the other migrant workers, he had firsthand knowledge of the poverty of the workers and of their illnesses as a result of overall living and working conditions plus the use of pesticides.

Although his early experience in school was harsh, he was avid in regard to education. He worked so that his children could go to college. He became the voice and champion for the migrant farmworkes, with the founding of the **UNITED FARM WORKERS** union in 1962. The challenges that they face to gain citizenship is an issue that can no longer go unresolved.

2016 – Some conditions appear to have lightened up a little. **2014** showed **45 million** at poverty level, down from the **49.7** in **2012.**

However there are at least 500,000 living in tent cities, including ***6,107 children under the age of 18.*** The homeless number has grown. On the news tonight the report re: "tent cities" said a site will be cleared and a larger one sets back up again. So far a solution has not been found in spite of the many coordinated efforts to solve the very large problem that has continued to escalate.

NOTE: But along with the above, we do have the money to house the criminals, (see pg. 125) and the federal government aid to schools, worldwide is at the low place of 137[th.]

THE POOR IN OUR COUNTRY: 2012 now stands at 49.7 million or 16% of the population. And the stock market is at an all-time high of 15,876.22; this, in the richest nation in the world. The homeless are numbered 633,782. This is one of the most disastrous statistics, in this land of so much wealth.

RAPE AND ABUSE

- **domesticviolence.org.** – Every nine seconds in the United States a woman is assaulted or beaten. Around the world, one in three women has been beaten, coerced into sex or other abuse during her lifetime.
- Every day in the U.S. more than three women are murdered by a husband or boyfriend. 92% of women listed domestic violence or sexual assault of top concern.
- Victims lost near eight million paid work days in the U.S. alone; equal to 32,000 full time jobs.
- Partner violence costs upward of $5.8 billion a year; $4.1 billion for direct care, $1.8 billion for lost productivity.
- Studies suggest that up to ten million children witness some form of domestic violence annually.

- Nearly one in five teenage girls who have had a relationship said the boyfriend threatened them or himself if they break up.
- Men, who as children see domestic violence growing up, are twice as likely to abuse their own wife, sons and daughters.
- Children under 18 months are the top victims resulting in 1,537 deaths in 2010; 79.4% were younger than four years, 47.7 percent under a year; girls 51.2% and boys 48.5%.
- Number of reports every year – 3.6 million; 81.2% of abusers a child knows are parent/caregiver, neighbors, friends or persons considered friends of the family.
- Age of perpetrators 36.3 (highest age group is 20-29 years of age).
- Report shows 45.2% are male, 53.6% female.

The following statistics are *CRITICAL*. Please note all very carefully.

Note: *The pornography industry is larger than the revenues of the top technology companies combined: Microsoft, Google, Amazon, eBay, Yahoo, Apple, Netflix, and Earthlink.*

Children Internet Porn Statistics

Average age of first exposure year	11
Largest age group years	35-49
15-17 years—multiple hard core exposure	80%
8-16 years – doing homework	90%
7-17 years – giving home address	29%

- Cildren's character names linked to thousands of porn links; 26 sites including Pokemon and Action Man
- Christians who said pornography is a major problem in the home 47%
- Breakdown of male/female visitors to porn sites: 72% male; 28% female.

~

PORNOGROPHY - familysafemedia.com

Top Five Countries

China	28%	
S. Korea	27%	
Japan	21%	
United States	**14%**	All others 10%

NOTE:
Every second -- $3,075.64 is spent on pornography
Every second–28,258 Internet users are viewing porn
Every second – 372 Internet users looking at research terms
***Every 39 minutes a new pornographic video is being created in the U.S.**

REVENUE AND PORNOGPHY

China	$27.4 billion	per capita:	$ 27.41
S. Korea	$25.7 billion	"	$526.76
Japan	$19.8 billion	"	$156.75
U.S.	$13.3 billion	"	$ 47.47

All others $ 86.2 billion (223 countries)

THIS AMOUNTS TO $94.82 BILLION -- $5.18 BILLION SHORT OF *ONE TRILLION DOLLARS*.

Yes, money has to be found to shut down this single most destructive force in our lives.

War on Drugs

- 30,000 are currently incarcerated for drug related crimes.
- Annual cost per inmate -- $31,286
- Or $10,324,380 per year
- Added: Police, court costs raises the figure to $40 billion a year; $400 billion over ten years.

NOTE: *To put the figure in perspective, the estimated cost of ending world hunger over the same ten year period would be $300 billion.*

Drug offenders constitute 48% of all federal inmates; by contrast, 7.6% are doing time for violent crimes. Next to pornography, WE HAVE TO GET CONTROL OF THE DRUG TRAFFICING.

Prisons (ipsnews.com)

- The United States has incarcerated far more people than any other country today, imprisoning 716 people out of very 100,000.
- 95,000 juveniles under 18 years of age were put in prison and that doesn't count for those in juvenile facilities.
- The U.S. has 5.6% of the world population and 25% of people incarcerated.
- Huffingtonpost: Guantanamo -- $900,000 per inmate.

PLEASE NOTE THE FOLLOWING STASTICTS

2016 – www.smartasset.com/insights/the-economy-of-the-American -prison-system Written by: Brian Kincade

In a the following article reported: The American Prison system is so vast it's estimated turnover of $74 billion eclipse the GDP OF 133 nations.

"What is (perhaps) most unsettling about this fact is that it is the American tax payer who foots the bill is increasingly padding the pockets of publicly traded like Corrections Corporation of America and GEO group, both companies combined, generated over $2.53 billion in 2012 and represents more than half of the private prison business."

~

As of January 1, 2016 the number of those who are on death row nation wide is:2,0943

2016 - I AM FOR THE DEATH PENALITY HE BEING REINSTATED:

The Families Of The Victems Are Entitled To Complete Closure For Memories Of What They Will Have To Live With For The Rest Of Their Lives , Especially The Children Whose Parent(s) Have Been Killed.

As Generations Pass, The Families Will Have The Consolation of Knowing That Justice Has Been Served. The Country Too, Will Regain The Knowledge That We Have Rightful Laws Back In Our Justice System. <u>The World Will Know That We Live In A Civilized Society, Where The Punishment Will Fit The Crime</u>

The following is how I arrived at method that can be developed automatically, where no one will have to live with the guilt that they were the one that was the direct source of a death.

Last night, on the 5:00p.m. news a story was aired about how to successfully rid New York City of rats. Dry Ice was put into a hole then covered up andsealed, so no air could get in. When thawed the ice turns to carbon dioxide and that solved the problem.

Today with this new discovery, I think this would be the most merciful way of euthanizing felons, who are on death row, because of their heinous crimes against their fellow humans.

With the advances in electronics, a system could be designed, without a single person being part of the process. The felon would have all of the: "last night" role still in place.

127

The next day, the person could be given a *light* sedation, strapped to a gurney and wheeled to the air tight chamber. Once inside the door would lock automatically.

With a dry system in place it would automatically melt by heat being applied for rapid evaporation, releasing the carbon dioxide. To clear the chamber oxygen would be forced in to clear the carbon dioxide. The door would then open automatically for thee room to be cleared.

Our Prison System Is The Largest In The World

2016 - www.salon.com/2012/10/15/us_has_more_prisoners

There are 2.2 million people currently in prison in the U.S. It is equal to the size of Houston noted Bloomberg News and we have 4,375 prisons currently, and that is 4 times the number of 2nd place Russia with 1,029.

PRISONERS WORLDWIDE

2016 – These figures are unchanged; indications are higher.

(Daily Liberty Forum 2/17/2011)

U.S	2,019,234		314,847,465 pop.
China	1,549,000	"	1,343,239,923 pop.
Russia	846,967	"	142,517,008 pop.
India	313,635	"	1,205,073,612 pop.
Brazil	208,204	"	193,946,886 pop.

The U.S. prison system costs the taxpayers $60 billion a year. This is another unnoted statistic of the cost to live here in America.

THESE ABOVE NEW NUMBERS LEAVE A PERONS NUMB. THERE ARE NO WORDS...
Impaired Driving Facts - cdc.gov. Motor vehicle safety.

Every day, almost 300 people in the U.S. die in motor vehicle crashes that involve an alcohol-impaired driver, one death every 48 minutes, at an annual cost of more than $51 billion.

In 2010, over 4.1 million drivers were arrested for driving under the influence of alcohol or narcotics.

Drugs other than alcohol (e.g., marijuana and cocaine) are involved in about 18% of motor vehicle deaths. **2016** – Cell phones on while driving: in 2013, there were 5.69 million car crashes; 1.2 million result of cellphones; 341, 000 texting while driving. No latest figures to date.

Most at risk: One out of three were between 21 and 24 years of age (34%). The next two largest groups: 15-34 (30%) and 35-44 (25%).

Nearly half of the alcohol-impaired motorcyclists killed each year are 40 or older.

Drivers with prior driving while impaired (DWI) convictions: Drivers with a blood alcohol content (BAC) of 0.08% or higher involved in fatal crashes were four times more likely to have a prior

2016 - NOTE: *SATANIC RITUAL ABUSE* **has surfaced again. Here in the state of Washington, this group has approached the School District to allow an after school activity led by them to** *OTHER WAY OF LOOKING AT OTHER RELIGIONS AND* conviction for DWI than drivers with no alcohol in their system.

MENTAL ILLNESS: Facts and Numbers – National Association of Mental Illness (NAMI) Reportne in four adults – approximately 57.7 million, Americans experienced a mental health disorder in a given year. One in 17 lives with serious mental illness, such as schizophrenia, major depression, or bipolar disorder and about one *in ten children live with serious mental or emotional disorders.*

About 2.4 million Americans or 1.1% of the adult population lives with schizophrenia.

Bipolar disorder affects 5.7 million American adults, approximately 2.6% of the adult population.

Major depressive disorder affects 6.7% of adults, or about 14.8 million American adults. According to the 2004 WORLD HEALTH REPORT, this is the leading cause of disability of ages 15-44 in the United States and Canada.

Anxiety disorders, including panic disorder, obsessive compulsive disorder (OCD), post-traumatic stress disorder (PTSD), and phobias affect about 18.7% of adults, an estimated 40 million individuals. Anxiety disorders frequently co-occur with depression or addiction disorders.

An estimated 5.2 million adults have co-occurring mental health and addiction disorders. Of adults using homeless services, 31% reported having a combination of these conditions.

One-half of all lifetime cases of mental illness begin by age 14, three-quarters by age 24. Despite effective treatments, there are long delays – sometimes decades – between the first onset of symptoms and when people seek and receive treatment.

Less than one-third of adults and one-half of children with a diagnosable mental disorder receive mental health services in a given year.

Racial and ethnic minorities are less likely to have access to mental health services, and often receive poorer quality of care.

In the United States, the annual economic, indirect cost of mental illness is estimated to be *$7 billion* a year.

Most of that amount – approximately $63 million – reflects the loss of productivity as a result of illnesses.

Individuals living with serious mental illness face an increased risk of having chronic medical conditions. Adults living with serious mental illness die 25 years earlier than other Americans, largely due to treatable medical conditions.

*Suicide is the eleventh-leading cause of death in the United States, **the third-leading cause of death for people age 10-24 years.** More* *than 90% of those who died by suicide have a diagnosable mental disorder.*

In July 2007, a nationwide report indicated that male veterans are twice as likely to die by suicide as compared with their civilian peers in the general United States population.

Twenty-four percent of state prisoners and 21% of local jail prisoners have a recent history of a mental health disorder. Seventy percent of youth in juvenile justice systems have at least one mental disorder with at least 20% with significant impairment from a serious mental illness.

Over 50% of students with a mental disorder age 14 and older drop out of high school – the highest dropout rate of any disability group.

ADOPTIONS: I cannot leave this section without commenting on the process of children that are up for adoption. I have firsthand information in regard to the case I want to share it with you. *It is all too typical and clearly shows that the person most affected—the child that is going into a permanent home and out of the system has*

NO RIGHTS AT ALL. I am pleading with all people working in the system to please give the welfare of the child, FIRST CONSIDERATION.

Here is this child's story. His mother is a drug addict and has two children; a ten year old girl and a three year old son, both by different fathers, and she has never been married. She has constantly broken probation through the past ten plus years. She is living with a family that includes the grandmother, mother and son in the family. The son is not the father of the girl, but claims her anyway as a member of the family. The ten year old sleeps in the same room as her "father." When the second child was born, the mother continued to live with this family. Because of the mother's history, DSHS finally took the child away from her and was placed in foster care, with a family known to this family.

This foster care family is 59-67 in age. They got the child when he was less than a year old. They had him for 17 months. Never in all of that time did the relatives of the mother make any attempt to contact the foster parents or make any kind of contact with the child. All of this time—for the past ten years the mother has been in and out of the courts and in detention for continually breaking probation. The court decided that the unknown "family" of the mother, who live out of state had first claim to adopt. More time passed. It turned out that they too, were ineligible.

The husband in the family fostering the child developed urinary cancer. As a result and because of the foster parent's ages, it was decided that the child would have to go back to foster care. A hearing is to be held this month to sever parental rights for both the mother and the fathers of the children. And then the boy will be available for adoption. And according to the then Supervisor, if all else is in place, the new family will be able to adopt the boy.

The day after Thanksgiving the family received a phone call from DSHS and was told that the boy was going to be flown out of state for three days to the birth mother's relatives. These people are considering adopting him. They have never had any children and have never seen the boy. A DSHS person, who the boy doesn't know, is going to take him on the flight east. The family was devastated.

Someone who is close to the situation called to talk with the supervisor. The previous supervisor was taken off of the case and the new one said that it is *always the case that the natural family be given first consideration.*

So this is where it stands. The burning questions, among others, are two: 1. If the mother will no longer have parental rights, why is the family being given first consideration? 2. And if they are given custody of the child and it doesn't work out, the child will wind up back in the system again. Would the family that want to adopt him still be able to? **THIS IS ABSOLUTELY INTOLERABLE.**

While the court was going back and forth about "rights, requirement, eligibility, and a welcoming home for the child, the new social worker was very diligent. She made connections with the family that wanted to adopt the child, this is the family that had wanted him from the begining It turned out to be an ideal situation.

They have strong Christian ideals and provide healthy guidelines for all of the children. The older two children's ages nine and six. This whole scenario was played out over a period of a year and a half. This child has been with them for over two months. A new name was chosen and is settled in and very happy. Another bonus is that he gets to see to older sibling, as time is worked out.

All that have eyes to read—what, when, where and why is all of this allow to happen? Imagine all of the children that are put in this position. Has everybody completely lost their minds? I hope this will raise a storm to heaven and right minded people will take a stand for this child and **250,000 children that go into foster care every year.**

QUESTION - handle Is it possible to have a separate entity to address specifically children issues? The Department of Health and Welfare Services has become to big to give the needed attention to are children. The Department could then be more ready to theialways overburden system. As I write this, I think a task force should examine all aspects of what is expected of them. By breaking down their overall responsibilities, time, money, and a streamlined system would be most beneficial to have need of their services. The parents would be most appreciative of knowing the all aspects of the needs of this special group will be handled under one roof.

~

To help children everywhere in the world, with all that they are subjected to, is it possible to have the many foundations, found a WORLD WIDE HEADQUARTERS under one umbrella?

It is imperative that all efforts to combat the PEDIPHILIC AND MURDEROUS

ELEMENT in the world, to combat this scourge that is decimating the most innocent of our population: <u>OUR CHILDREN?</u>

~

SECULAR ACTIVITIES." This story was on our 5:00 o'clock news in mid-August. I urgently asked that all parents go on the web and bring up all information you can find, so we can make a concerted effort to finally get this out in the open. CAUTION: The finger pointing at the Catholic Church, however going through the web pages, almost all organized groups that work with children have been targeted including many religions, and secular groups. I found these three reputable, accurate sites:

<u>www.endritiualabuse,org/ritualabusearchive.htm</u>

<u>www.psychologytoday,com/blog/do-the-right-2012-06</u>

<u>www.ritualabuse.us/ritualabuse/articles</u>

2016 – Today September 16. I feel compelled to repeat these two events.

The first story reminds me of the book written in 1983 by William Golding, a British novelist, playwright and poet won the Nobel Prize in Literature for his works including: "The Lord Of The Flies," for his body of works dealing with the human condition.

"The Lord Of the Flies" is the story of two groups of boys, between the ages of 8 and 13/14 living at a boys school in England, where one group has dominance over the other group."

This morning, on Facebook was a picture of a beautiful, innocent 9 year old boy, smiling in the warm sunshine. The caption under the picture: "Did this boy commit suicide because of bullying?"

This story especially caught my attention today, because *it is the third time this year* that these tragedies have occurred, that I have learned of, through the media.

This is another dismal sign of the deterioration that has now become part of the American pattern among children. Law and order has rapidly slipped through our legal and judicial systems. Will we lose it all this November 8, 2016, when we elect a new President?

~

This story on our 5 o' clock news:

This next story is makes a person PROUD TO BE AND AMERICAN.

We have made general strides in that our black population is now a vital part of our society. *But racial profiling has not abated.*

One of the grade schools (1st through 6th) in our state decided that they would involve the children in THE BLACK LIVES MATTER movement sweeping the country, protesting the near epidemic proportions of brutality, nationwide.

They had the shirts made up for all sizes, printed up and the day was set. The event was video was taped. You could feel the energy in the air.

The tape showed the children with their shirts on, along with their backpacks. As they approached the front door of the school, with the parents encouraging this march, they were met with a long cordon of black people lined up with their hands outstretched.

As the children approached the entry, their arms outstretched from their shoulders, they walked ahead, hands meeting hands. The children were very enthusiastic as they walked through the cordon,

135

the next game to be held another protest would take place. Feathers were ruffled again has to how it would unfold.
The coach of the team, managed to get the situation under control and the game went on with the player on the field too They knew this was the right thing to do. It was a tremendous and heart touching moment.

Afterward some of the parents were interviewed. All had big smiles on their faces and proud of their children.

This event was a singular moment in and of itself. It is a story of good upbringing and faith. Prior to this walk for BLACK LIVES MATTER, this story is a remarkable story in, and of itself. {It takes on global proportions when parents encourage this type demonstration, especially in the toxic climate in our country today.}

2016 - THESE DEMONSTRATION IS WHAT WE KNOW AND LOVE ABOUT AMERICA. This is what America is about; peaceful demonstrations calling attention to what is wrong in America today. It takes on added significance when the children are involved. It is only in a Democratic form of government that we can show how much we care, for the concerns and issues that have arisen, among our diverse population. Always join and support these activities as they arise. Justice is served for all our people when the voice of the people is heard.

Another black protest happened over these last two weeks. A player on one of the teams in the NFC – West, in the opening game of this year's football season, sat through the singing of our National Anthem.

Loud debate on both sides weighed the pros and cons of his actions. His actions left questions in many people's mines, because in all of our sports, the one area where the only interest is "the game."

To date, no controversy has been aroused inside of what happens in the sports arena. People took the incident in stride, as we do, until a black player on another team, indicated that at.

At the end of the game, which they won, the whole team and managers, with the coach in the middle, stood across the field, all arms locked together and stood in unity. This was another proud moment in our history: this is The American way. Go... on and on an....

2016 - POLICE BRUTALITY: Has reached near epidemic proportions today. Police department and agencies across our country have created many tasks forces to curb this violence and to date, have not been unable to bring the police brutality under control.

It is the types of provocation that are non-life threatening, and people are killed, because of a weapons be considered "lethal." A rock throwing occurred in our state recently. The man that was killed was running away from three policemen, after he had thrown rocks at them, hitting two.

www.nbcnews.com/us-news/pasco **February, 2015**

NBC News reported on the shooting in Pasco, WA. A Mexican worker was shot at 17 times, after a being chased by three police, for throwing rocks, hitting two of them, but no injuries were reported, by them. He was hit five times. In a film clip of the incident, the victim had turned and was facing the police, while running away from the police, when he was shot. There were three other shootings in a seven month period. (More on the web.)

Automatically, when a police shooting occurs in our state, the police involved are on paid administrative leave. There have been too many cases that have been reviewed, where the, the ruling is in favor of the police.

This is one of the key issues today. The enormity of this issue, to cover all aspects of why, requires those who have the knowledge to give a concise scope of their findings.

As a result of the legislation that has been passed relaxing regulation, *it appears this has given those in "authority" to abuse and license to "shoot first then answer."* This is one more reason we have to regain control of what direction our country will go.

COMMUNISM: Continued From Back Cover.

2016 – NOTE: 1950's McCarthyism ran amuck calling citizens from the government..., army..., movie industry..., or who came from various backgrounds and walks of life... when appearing before Congress had to answer to: "Are you now or have you ever been a member of the Communist party?"

A witch hunt ensued and the nation was torn apart and finally it came to an end in the middle 1950s. "Communist," was cut from the national political language and was substituted with the word "Socialist." Today it is a different name, but is still the identical stripe.

www.Amarillo.com>opinion>Leters to the editor. October 8, 2012

Khrushchev Prediction: Slowly Communism has worked through our system:

"We will take America without firing a shot. We can't expect America to jump from Capitalism to Communism... we can assist their elected leaders by giving small doses of Socialism... one day... they will have Communism.

www.wikipedia.org/wiki/socialist_party

The Communist Party has their head-quarters: A J Muste building in New York City, NY

Communism is alive and well in America. People in public office who are registered as a Socialist are members of the Communist party: also known as Socialist Party USA or Socialist Party

www.wikipedia.org/kshamaswant

We have one Socialist member on the Seattle City Council, Kshama Sawant. She moved to Seattle in 2006. She was a part time teacher at Seattle Central Community College. The position was not renewed.

2013 she won a seat on the Council. She was the activist. In the forefront, for the $15.00 an hour, minimum wage, she was not happy when she learned that it will take three years on graduated tiers to implement this new legislation. But "we won" she said after the final vote was counted. She represents the poor, immigrants, refugees and "the folks not represented on the City Council." She was born in India.

So the question remains: Are the Koch brothers working with the Communist Party, or are they acting on their own and the Communist have used what the Kochs have accomplished in the last 43 years to their advantage.

Headlines have been publishing news about active Fascism, in the country. Is this another smoke screen to hide the activities of the communist in our country? Recently weeks, the former chairman of the Trump campaign stepped down, because of his connection, with a person in the Russian government. The President is concerned about this turn of events.

And still the question remains. We do know that subversive elements are at work to undermine this election. Will they be successful? The above illustrates known Communist are very active in American Politics and have been, since the Bolshevik Revolution. If we lose our Democracy, you can depend that we will all be answering to a totalitarian government and the police will be the one to enforce the new regulations of the regime. Their efforts started 99 years ago, with the Bolshevik Revolution, October, 2017.

VALUABLE DISCUSSIONS ON
DOMESTIC ISSUES

"The most certain test by which we judge
whether a country is really free is the amount
of security enjoyed by the minorities."

Lord Action (John E. E. Delberg)
English Historian

SCHOOLS – The First Place To Start

It is in our schools, from pre-school forward the centers of learning must teach and demonstrate the value of Democracy. Our schools, along with so many of our programs to teach and help those in need, are two areas that have been hardest hit, in the cuts of the federal programs underwriting these essentials to a sound and Safe Democracy. I am hoping that the following points will generate serious discussions.

Revamp the whole system by testing all new incoming students attending school for the first time to determine at what level they should start. Compose classes of

those students that fall in three categories.

1. Basic **2.** Intermediate **3.** Advanced: The level to be determined by test scores. Teachers that determine a student should be in another level, show support of her findings with the student's work and a general test of overall knowledge to move up to a higher level.

The stigma of "failing" would be removed. All students will progress when working at the level where they are best suited. Candidates from this level could continue with further education in an area best suited to help them in the job market.

Behavior problems in the advanced levels should also be taken into consideration. Educators should be able to find solutions to bridge this factor.

BIRTH CONTROL AND ABORTION

Limited abortion in cases of the life of the mother and proven cases of rape and severe medical challenges. The state of Kansas's bill states that: 'Life begins 'at fertilization'. **2016 -** It must become the standard for all and the only way we are to regain our moral compass.

NOTE: I agree with this position. Everything in nature that is growing started from a seed or cell. When seeds are planted and tended, they grow. We can all see living vegetation including food as a result.   No one questions the beginning of life in the animal/aquatic world. Nothing can grow if it doesn't have life.

Young people of both sexes that are of the age to engage in sexual activity and results in the partner getting pregnant *should not be able to have an abortion.* They have to be held responsible for their sexual license. Ban morning after pills for all *under the age of 18. Free and over the counter pills promotes early sexual activity.*
*** *(As of today 4/30/2013) 'the pill will be available to anyone over the age of 15 without parents' consent. NO CHILD SHOULD HAVE TO SUFFER THE CONSEQUENCES OF IRRESPONSIBLE PARENTS. From the very beginning of their lives, they are deprived of living in a caring, loving, and stable home. We must put this issue in the top priority. We must remove a historical pattern of repetition by allowing the law to continue to stand.*

ROE v. WADE: Justice Ruth Ginsberg has said that this law is too broad: The Supreme Court needs to revisit and revise with more stringent legislation. *Morality cannot be legislated, but we can include language that puts the responsibility back where it belongs.*

Exception to Roe v. Wade to include:

No reimbursement for "unwanted pregnancies." It is my personal view that a mere child up to age 13 should be made to carry the baby until term. Their bodies are not fully developed. (This is an area that I have no knowledge and is strictly forbidden by our Catholic Church, that I am a member of) but in the political climate in our country today, from this age forward and upward, unwanted pregnancies have to be paid for by the person/family responsible for the dependent child. All efforts should be made to hold the person responsible and his family, should share the costs. *If there is a repeat of the procedure, a criminal penalty should be attached.*

We citizens should not be penalized by paying for this permissive behavior. Nor should society have to support these unwanted children. The people that bring these children into the world get off scot free and the government (*We The People*), are left to address this issue and deal with all of the attendant problems for all of those who fall into this category, and allow the continuing culture of permissiveness.

We need to educate the young and troubled children of the outcome of sexual activity and to stress that they will not under law, be able to get an abortion without parental consent. Medical plans should not provide coverage for the pregnancies and current abortions in healthy young women. Starting in junior high school, mandatory classes need to be included in the curriculum to give accurate information about the outcome of early activity. Parents must be held responsible for their children's activities.

We will not turn the tide of this rampant, promiscuous, immoral behavior that is prevalent in our society today, until we parents call for a change in the climate that promotes this behavior through uncensored entertainment mediums.

2016 - Morality cannot be legislated but legislation and regulations have a moral obligation to formulate the narrowest interpretation of what is passed. The lack of regulations that are now in place, promote promiscuity, leading to a further breakdown of the basis of society. The pharmaceutical colossus is the first place to start.

In writing the following, I am clear about people being raped, but it is an example that leaves a person to question some cases classified as rape.

A long number of years ago a young lady aged 18 filed a law suit for being raped. The testimony that came out in court showed that she voluntarily went to the hotel room of the person charged with the rape. The time was 3:00 a.m. She won the case. Rape needs to be proven in cases. Why was this young woman going to this hotel at 3:00 a.m. alone? Education in this area is imperative.
How did the Court decide it was rape? As I recall, this person was a sports figure and had prior convictions. Even if this young woman did not know of his history, she should have been considered old enough at the age of 18 to know not to go alone to

his room at 3:00 a.m. We have to stop excusing poor judgment and bad behavior.

I am all for two young people to move in together, if they make a commitment to each other. The conditions would have to be that, after a year, they set a wedding date or move on with their lives. I don't know how many would agree with this possibility. As I have stated, I practice my Catholic religion, but the statistics today tell the tale of children from divorced parents. This area is another one of our major challenges today in re-establishing strong family values.

If a young couple cannot handle the challenges that arise in this one year trial period, they certainly will not be able to withstand the major challenges that come into all lives. The good news, I see a trend among the young people toward building friendships first. As more and more people marry their true friend, marriage stability will right itself.

In today's environment, the first place young women *and* young men can start to change this pattern is by the way they dress and think seriously about what actions and habits suggest he/she is available by being too friendly. This is part of the education that needs to be strongly included. Getting spiritual values and guidance active in young lives will be one of the quickest ways for young people to learn 'where to draw the line'. An old adage is as relevant today as when it was first uttered: *Familiarity breeds contempt.*

Send a message to the clothing and accessories industries to have more becoming and less suggestive apparel. Leave *something* to the imagination. Doctor Oz has done a thorough job of showing how we are all put together inside. We have seen enough nudity to know what we look like on the outside, and it isn't all that interesting. What do you think—*maybe*—just maybe, the fashion industry would stand the fashion world on its ear and vie for who produces designs that have the most *overall* appeal.

2016 – LGBT COMMUNITY: The country is having to adjust to this latest change in our social structure. A cursory review of what is known about homosexuality has still not come up with any conclusive findings. Research aside, this community has grown very large. Generally speaking, it is becoming enculturated into society including same sex marriage. Many of this group were married heterosexually and are raising their children in a single gender family unit. Because this a very recent development, the effects on children in this new environment has not shown evidence about the effects that it having on these children. So far, nothing noteworthy has been reported.

This community has had many documented studies. In my view, it falls into the category of an aberration of nature. Now that the LGBT has been sanctioned, *many stories* from couples that have lived their lives under the radar no longer live in the shadows of society. Committed relationships are now sanctioned by being to repeat the marriage vows.

My observations are: that this is the hardest aspect to accept. However, problems have arisen when one of the couple die, they are entitled to benefits of their partner, that they have shared their lives with. Marriage has eliminated this obstacle and now the survivor has equal rights, under the law and all benefits resulting from these unions go to the survivor.

Some of the Christian voting block are most critical of the LGBT community, following the guidelines of the Bible. Homosexuality has a recorded history from ages past. The greater religious opinion is mixed, however many of the major religions, while not allowing the validity of these marriages, do show their compassion and ask for blessings and prayers for all. We too, should offer our prayers and remember "judge and so you will be judged."

2016 – "*Soft Porn is now is almost unnoticed.* And today, we have seen pictures of the wife, of an aspiring candidate for the Presidency of the United States of America: *POSING IN THE NUDE. I don't call this soft porn and all children can be exposed to this and other ways that have become too common to get control of the minds and lives.*

AVERTISING: the movie industry and television all promote all goods and services that have sex appeal from what we wear to what is shown as acceptable behavior at the Super Bowl. All of these mediums use highly lewd material depending on the medium they operate in.

A very graphic illustration of a lewd example was displayed during this year's half-time ceremony. It is very apparent this group of young women have had insufficient or no education for their responsibility to the people younger than themselves to show the beauty of dance, rather than this display. A picture with the following caption was printed the following day. *"... The half-time show brought plenty of girl power to the testosterone-laden...performance."*

This is a target of exploitation by the entertainment industry and it does not fall into the porn category as it should. Good money is paid to see this type entertainment in the capital of entertainment, Nevada. It is up to us to make change happen.

Statistics show the devastation taking place in our country.
2016 - None of this has changed and according to the news these problems have escalated.

- Multiple drug cartels moving into the heartland and embedded in our country.
- Alcohol and drug abuse results in the slaughter on our highways.
- The number of felons and prisons are full, allowing lighter sentences or being shortened or suspended, for lack of room.
- Domestic violence, child abuse and pornography that is devastating our innocent young worldwide
- The NRA/gun lobby. *These statistics can no longer be tolerated.* It has been shown that in many areas, the United States is the most violent nation in the western world.
- Remove the race question from all forms; if people are citizens, this designation should be removed. An internal code can be put into place *under limited, restricted*

146

conditions. We are all American citizens and should be treated equally.

SOCIAL SECURITY: This benefit should be restricted to households whose earnings do not exceed $200,000 a year. When Social Security was established during the Great Depression in 1929/1930's, the intent was to provide those who retired without retirement benefits and for those who sustained disabilities that cut their earning capabilities before retirement age. If a person's income is above this level, they certainly don't' need the government to turn on this spigot for more. An audit in this area would certainly turn up some interesting information

RE: GAYS: as adult leaders of youth groups; this whole issue is too new and will take time to be accepted. Great strides have been made in their behalf.

REMINDER: The *African American* community had to wait 100 years after the Civil War to be granted freedom, after 300 hears. It took another 100 years, starting in the 1960's for the second bloody years of violence to finally attain equal status with all Americans. Although not at the virulent level of the 1960's, racism is still alive and well her in America.

BOY SCOUTS: The recent decision of the Boy Scouts of America to not allow gay leaders of youth groups is now in place. These new regulations come within their structure, to further nourish our youth in the moral and ethical values, plus the sacredness of the family structure as defined by *Spiritual Law.* The gay issue will remain with individual circumstances when this choice is made.

SEX EDUCRTION: There was a time when sex education for all children was not considered appropriate before the early teen years. Now children are learning "the facts of life" from anyone (including some teachers and parents) who decides to "fill them in." This, too, has contributed in earlier participation in promiscuous activity.

PHARMACEUTICAL COMPANIES: No wonder the pharmaceutical companies say that prevention should be sold to anyone of any age 'without parental consent'—the bottom line in business you know; that's what keeps their stocks viable in the stock market.

TODAY'S BIG QUESTION

DIFFERENCE OF VIEWS – Individual Rights vs. Collective Rights *When does the minority rights take precedence over the majority rights? In these last fifty years, more and more of our sacred and treasured values have been eroded because of this precedent that is practiced today, granting individual rights at the expense of* majority.

ACLU: All of these years later we are seeing the results of these decisions. The **ACLU** history started in 1925 and has made similar inroads into the downturn in the quality of our way of life. My hope is that by citing these few instances, it will encourage people with expertise in law take a look at the whole body of law since the early 20th century.

This is a law that needs to be overturned NOW. I am surprised that the ACLU hasn't tried to overturn all of our Constitution. Our Founding Fathers and the people that came here to settle our country came for RELIGIOUS FREEDOM. ISLAM is the latest religion that is allowed to be practiced in some states but not all. This is another instance where the rights of the few, take precedence over the majority.

OATH OF ALLEGIANCE

When new citizens take the Oath of Allegiance in the process of becoming Americans, they leave behind all of their former laws that they adhered to and agree that the laws of our country will be the laws they live by. As in all relationships--one on one, communities and countries, it is the give and take that keeps the strength of all associations and creates the bond that promotes the American way.

Because individual rights have been given first consideration status, our ethical and moral values have been weakened and it shows in the daily fabric of our lives. A code of laws are only as good as they apply for the good of all of the people...knowing that some people will not be in agreement. It balances out for everyone however, as all people do not accept the same values as others at the same time. These principles were set at the beginning of human history as individuals found that they have a stronger voice collectively.

When the few have more say than the majority, deterioration sets in. By working with the minority view we can find a middle ground. This is the one of the principles of our Constitution. These issues need to be revisited if we are to regain BALANCE in our NATIONAL LIFE.

~

PIVITOL DECISIONS

May, 1954, Brown v. Board of Education, ends school segregation and June, 1966 Miranda v. Arizona: Reading Rights, the decision in January,

July, 1989 - Allegheny County v. Greater Pittsburgh ACLU: Christian Nativity Scene violates the Establishment clause. The Nativity Scene is not allowed, but the Chanukah Menorah is.

June, 1997 - Reno v. ACLU - Restriction on Free speech to protect minors from indecent material on TV. ACLU prevailed.

NOW: In my view, the Supreme Court has taken the point of the letter of the law and not allowing for the intent of the law. The result has been that by these narrow interpretations, they have slowly eroded our freedoms. The decisions handed down from the Supreme Court set the tone for interpretation of the law, and the lower courts and the judicial system have followed suit.

ANOTHER pivotal case in the history of the country was the cast of the vote in **Bush v. Gore, December, 2000,** giving Bush the Presidency. A short 13 years later, we are all too clear about this decision. The important point in this case is that "eight days earlier, in the case of Supreme Court case Bush v. Palm Beach County Canvassing Board, has unanimously decided a closely related case and only three days earlier had preliminarily halted a recount that was occurring."

This past President's holiday, I was talking with one of my younger granddaughter's; I asked her if she knew why this national holiday was being celebrated. She said "no." I then asked if she knew who President Lincoln was; again "no." She is in the third grade. What happened to all of those stove pipe hats and the fallen cherry tree...the school boy, George Washington said: "I cannot tell a lie."

Other areas of controversy that are basic to our freedom include:
 That all are allowed to practice their religious beliefs.
- Oregon has limited these rights in their schools.
- Do all schools take a moment for silent prayer after the Pledge of Allegiance is recited?

Believers of all faiths acknowledge a Higher Power and I am sure parents teach their children to show reverence and respect for their religious ceremonies. For those who are non-believers, it is a way these families can teach their children to say THANK YOU for known benefits of nature and to be able to acknowledge that life does have its benefits. It is these little reminders throughout the day that keep moral values in life in the front of their minds, where they should be. I feel quite certain that non-believers do enjoy life.

Why can't all people express themselves as they see fit during the holidays? We Christians haven't determined what we feel are appropriate use of displays during this time of the year. Isn't Free Speech all inclusive? *The ACLU brought the issue of the Nativity Scene in public places to be banned (because it was/is against the sensitivities of non-believers).* So like prayer in school, now we who pledge One Nation, Under God are proscribed from public display of our beliefs.

I would like to see not just during the Christmas season, *but* also all year. If they had more public recognition given through public displays, then we too, can give greetings to those who celebrate their heritage, including Hanukkah, and Kwanza

This Muslim celebration is held the first week of December. **www.kumc.edu/diversity/ethnic** It is a sacrificial recommitment of obedience to God, following the example set by Ibrahim's obedience to God and a day of sharing with those that do not have as much. *Light and remembrance unite all of these celebrations.* The websitehas six pages showing the celebrations throughout the year.

Kwanzaa is a beautiful celebration with "the lighting of black, red and green candles celebrating the seven basic values of African American family life which include: Unity, Self-determination, Collective Work and Responsibility, Cooperative Economics, Purpose, Creativity and Faith."

These are the following for December: Ashura – Islamic, Muslim – 5th; St. Nicholas Day – International – 6th; Bodhi Day –Buddha's Enlightenment – 8th; Hanukkah – 8-16th; Virgin of Guadalupe – Mexico -12th; Santa Lucia Day – Sweden – 13th; Las Posadas – Mexico – 16-25th; Christmas – Christian, Roman Catholic, International – 25th, (Eastern Orthodox – celebrated in January); Boxing Day – Canada, United Kingdom – 26th; Kwanzaa – African American – 26th.

I can't help but wonder if the heritage days of celebration for all people have been dampened by the rulings sponsored by the **ACLU.**

THE VALUE OF SPIRIT
IN OUR DAILY LIVES

Your neighbor is in the
image and likeness of God.
"Love Your Neighbor as
You Love Yourself."
Romans 13:9

"God has died in the transcendent form and reality
and is now fully incarnate in every face and
human hand.   It is a way of saying that Christ
lives more fully and comprehensively now
than He has ever lived before."

Thomas J.J. Altizer
Professor of Religion,
Emory University

SPIRIT IN OUR DAILY LIVES

God Is Not Dead

I believe in the sun
even though it is
not shining.

I believe in love
even though
I feel it naught.

I believe in God
even though
He is Silent.

Found on some Walls in
bombed out Europe after World
War II.

"Live everyday as it were your last."

Prayer to Spirit

Come Glorious Spirit
Fill all hearts
With the power of
Your Divine Love,

Send forth Your Spirit and
You shall renew the face
Of the earth.

Webster's New World Dictionary – Third College Edition -- Definition of the word catholic; 1. general scope or value; all inclusive; **universal**; 2. broad in sympathies, taste or understanding; liberal, etc...

The purpose of starting this section with the definition is to show that the word **catholic has a very broad meaning.** It has been my experience that many people associate the word catholic, only with the Catholic Church. Catholicism is the source of my spiritual foundation. It is the first and foremost source of how I practice my interactions with all people.

Your spiritual foundation is of equal importance. God did not intend for all people to live in one house. (Can you imagine it? I don't want to.) When I was teaching catechism to the public school 7th and 8th graders, I used to tell them: *Do not be critical of anyone's belief system; they are like the spokes in a bicycle wheel, they all go to the same hub.*

The values of exchange between people, one on one but spreading out further, group to group, community to community, always reaching to extend out into the world further and further. It is through these exchanges that we enlarge our knowledge and grasp the simplicity and complexity of all of us that live in the world. The exchange of thoughts that result in consensus, make all of us better and stronger as a people. As we get to know each other the bonds between us grow too. So while I use my experience as a person of

154

the Catholic faith to reach out to others, in no way would I ever negate another's values.

The Power of Prayer

We Christians have many houses of worship. That is how it should be. There is not one house in the world that can hold the whole human race. God gave man the right to live as he chooses. The choices that man has made from the beginning of time, has resulted in the world as we know it today. Acceptance of life as it is, in its present state, presents us with the opportunity to improve on all that has been established before us.

Respect and acceptance of each person's place in life, how they live, and what they believe, is a mark of each individual's makeup. Look for the qualities that you admire and learn from them. We are teachers to each other. Everyone has warts, or are they just some of their particular characteristics?

Friendship is based on acceptance of the whole person. The majority of people are basically good. Everyone carries the way they were taught about the basics in life throughout their lives. By learning how a person was raised, their belief systems, and manner of doing things, is really the key to people getting along with others. It is the human condition and through friendship, it is easy to see these differences as just that.

The best values of exchange between people start by accepting a person, one on one, then group to group, community to community and then out into the world further and further. I had the good fortune in 1984 to attend the dress rehearsal for the upcoming summer Olympics. After the rehearsal was over, all stood for a standing ovation. There were many there from around the world. The most moving moment was when spontaneously we reached out and held hands clear around the stadium. I will never forget that moment.

It is through these exchanges that we enlarge our knowledge and grasp the simplicity and complexity of all of us that live in this world. The exchange of thoughts that result in consensus, make all

155

of us better and stronger as people. As we get to know each other the bonds between us grow too.

In all recorded history, there is no record of anyone who asked to be born:

Or into the family he was born into,
Or the country where he was born,
Or his race,
Or the color of his skin,
Or the way he was raised,
Or rich,
Or poor,
Or given talents,
Or lack of ability,
Or one's belief system in God/Spirit or a Higher Power.

We are the whole human race, all breathing the same air, enjoying the same sunshine, fresh air and rain, and all recognizing a higher Source.

Through the means of worldwide travel, we have a golden opportunity today to get to know our whole human family and embrace them as brother and friend. When you receive blood from the blood bank, none of the above information is attached regarding the donor, only the blood type. This is a true act of love for our fellow man, to give another life through a transfusion. With the advances in medicine, we now know that every individual has his own unique DNA. Our DNA identifies each and every one of us as individuals from the beginning of time.

Let us respect all people we meet remembering the **Golden Rule:** *"Do unto others as you would have them do unto you."*

Also, Jesus said: "Why do you see the speck in your brother's eye and not the beam in your own...do not judge, for with your judgment you will be judged..." (Matthew 7:1). The God-given breath of life is in each and every one of us.

A very wise priest told us: We cannot know why some things occur. Better than carrying all of the hurt inside, put it into a box

156

and label it FOR GOD TO HANDLE. Put the box on the shelf and let God handle what we cannot. I have found that the box always has room for more. There are some things we are not supposed to understand. When we turn it over to God, we acknowledge our faith is in His eternal wisdom.

At this time, the world is in a very precarious state. It is not the end of the world that has been in existence for a billion years or more; the end of the world for each one of us is when we no longer exist. Major threats have surfaced again. There is no way we can soften the message and now is the time to strengthen the human connection.

For all of our world family who hold other beliefs, we must respect their creeds. We are all one people in our diversity and all come from the same source. In our church, the body stands as the metaphor for the church; Christ is the head, we the people are the parts of the body.

This is a particularly good analogy. On a worldwide scale, we all make up the whole body because we are all brothers and sisters. Each nation and its people are vital to the whole world. If a part or system fails, the body will not be able to function properly as a whole. Each and every one of us throughout the world has an important part in the human ecosystem.

Wikipedia.org shows that 73-76% of Americans are Christian, 15-20% other, and 6+% agnostic or atheist, yet states that only 17% attend church on a regular basis, while some surveys show 40% attendance, but not on a regular basis. It is known that attendance on a regular basis is down.

Some of the reasons are the changes in the demographics of churches that accept the new lifestyle changes. The section on Family Life in America showed the deterioration in the basic values because of domestic violence, drugs, and crime.

Let families learn together that each of us in our own way need to take a few minutes each day (preferably in the morning), to say THANK YOU for the gift of life and ask for blessings for this new day. Everything that we have is from our Creator. A simple thought is that all our efforts for the day will become a prayer when the intention is for our fellow people and their trials. People do the same for you. At night before going to bed (with the children if at home) say THANK YOU for this day and have a prayerful rest. Later in life, children will treasure this source of inspiration and comfort.

To gain full confidence in this connection with Spirit, find time for meditation and reflection. It is the quickest refreshment you will find, especially after a very hectic day. Even though our lifestyles have changed and many do not adhere to the guideposts that are there, we all can take the right turn and ask for Divine guidance in our lives. You will be amazed at how all of the pressing problems will smooth out. As time goes by, the time will come when you will turn more and more to prayer and know the peace that only Spirit can give. Life here on earth is a journey to our eternal home.

During one of his crusades, the Reverend Dr. Billy Graham gave us his concept of God:

> God is like the wind;
> You can hear it; You can feel it;
> You can see the effects of it,
> But you can't see the wind itself.

2016 – Franklin Graham has stepped in to the shoes of his father Dr. Billy Graham an is touring the country this election year. His message is published in the September, 2016 issue: **DECISION,** a publication of the **Billy Graham Evangelistic Association.**

The article **"Billy Graham On CHRISTIAN Civic Duty** reprises "my father' words from a 1952 interview with Christian Life magazine, are more timely than ever. His challenging words speak of the need for Christian engagement in politics." In the words of Billy Graham: I think it is the duty of every individual Christian at election time to study the issues and candidates and then go to the polls and vote."

This message does, loudly resonate today. It is through the voting booth, where our voices are heard. *Especially in such a critical election in America.* Past elections have shown that if people are "TURNED OFF" as we are today only a small percentage go to the polls. And this is why we are in the downward spiral now and how this rogue element was able to gain there ends.

This pattern, of not voting, because "you are disgusted, or don't like the candidates", is what has enabled them to put their candidates into office since 1973. With their candidates, now in key positions, in all levels of government, they implemented the laws and policies drawn up in secret meetings, through their organization: America Legal Exchange Council (ALEC). They are depending on this pattern to continue.

This election is the most crucial since the Civil War, 248 years ago. If we are going to save our Democracy, this vote on November 8, 2016 must be the largest on record to date, to reject this oligarchy, who has 107 offices around the world, with intention of one rule, world-wide. If we have a poor turn out our Democracy will be swept away. And this will be the end of the promise made 55 years ago, President John F. Kennedy.

WE HAVE AND OBLIGATION TO OURSELVES, OUR CHILDREN, OUR COUNTRY AND THE WORLD TO "PUT AN END TO THIS GREATEST THREAT, THAT COULD TUMBLE DEMOCRACIES ALL OVER THE WORLD, RESULTING INA WORLD WIDE DICTATORSHIP, SO THAT A NEW SOCIAL ORDER CAN BE FORMED. EVERY VOTE COUNTS, ONE VOTE AT A TIME. GO TO THE POLLS NOVEMBER 8TH AND VOTE TO SAVE OUR DEMOCRACY.

GETTING IN THE GAP was written by Dr. Wayne W. Dyer, an internationally renowned author and speaker in the field of self-development. He is a great feature on PBS television and how I first became acquainted with Dr. Dyer and his lifelong work.

The following is on the jacket of his book: "Through meditation, we can tap into an abundance of creative energy that resides within us, and a more meaningful experience of life, which enriches us permanently."

I was especially taken with his commentary on listening: "...take the letters that make up the word *listen* and rearrange them so that they spell out "silent;--listen/silent the same in content only arranged to appear different from each other." When you listen you'll feel silence. When you're silent, you'll hear at a new level of listening... " Further in this paragraph: "...listen *with* silence."

Note that the word *silence* and the word *license* also have the exact letters as well. "Silence gives you a license to listen and be silent simultaneously."

THE THREE LEAF CLOVER: When he arrived in Ireland around 400 A.D., inspiration came to St. Patrick and he used the three-leaf clover as an example to explain the Triune God – Father, Son and Holy Spirit in which we now believe; three separate complete leaves on one stem; the triune God – God The Creator, God the Son, and God the Spirit that leads us today, as embodied in Jesus.

This is the reason the Irish celebrate Saint Patrick's Day. Life in these United States includes BIG PARTIES and on Saint Patrick's it is an unspoken national holiday—a party day. No one is going to denigrate a good party. But I also think it helps to know that not all of the Irish start to celebrate St. Patrick's Day until they first thank God for having this gift of the explanation of Three Persons in one God as Saint Patrick used a shamrock for an explanation. That is why the shamrock is so important to the Irish; it is a symbol of our faith in One God, Three Divine Persons, Father the Creator, Son the Savior, and the Holy Spirit – our guide and inspiration (in-*spirit).

~

Thoughts for Meditation

Romans 5:3-5 – We boast in hope of the glory of God. Not only that, by faith we even boast of our afflictions, knowing that affliction produces endurance, and endurance, proven character, and proven character, hope, and hope does not disappoint because the love of God has been poured out into our hearts through the Holy Spirit that has been given to us.

~

Today, many question the existence of God. God is not dead, rather we have abandoned God. God always has been, always is, always will be. This is important to think about: Where did creation come from? From matter; where did the matter come from?

Yes, science has developed the ability to *clone*, but where did the material come from. It has never been attempted or discussed (to my limited knowledge) that no one can wring their hands or wave a wand and produce *something.* They had the material to work with.

~

Before creation there was silence.

~

"I am the Alpha and the Omega, the beginning and the end", says the Lord God, "who is and who was and who is coming, the Almighty" (Rev. 1:8).

~

"Then the Lord, God formed man out of the dust of the ground and breathed into the nostrils then man became a living being." **(Genesis 2:)**

~

The breath of life is the breath of God, passed to each one, such as one candle to another. The breath of life is the spark of life. A newly born baby cries in the process of being born; the crying made possible because of the breath of life.

~

Why does life cease when breath leaves the body? Where does the breath go?

~

"For gold is tried by fire and acceptable men in the furnace of adversity." **(Wisdom 3:6)**

~

161

Merton

"We must make the choices that enable us to fulfill the deepest capacities of our real selves."

"Faith is the continual demonstration of the strength and wonder of life."   Thomas Merton

"God's Will Knows No Why"

– On the ring of Mother Superior from the book TRAPP FAMILY SINGERS – Maria Von Trapp told us in her book.

~

"Gratitude is the salve that heels the wounds of negligence."

~

"Ignorance Is Bliss – until reality sets in."

~

"There are no new thoughts, but there are enlighten ones."

~

We Share Our Faith Through, Prayer, Poetry and Song

"In this manner you shall pray." (Matthew 6:9)

Our Father, who art in heaven, Hallowed be thy name. Thy Kingdom come, thy will be done, on earth as it is in Heaven. Give us this day our daily bread and forgive us our trespasses, as we forgive those who trespass against us, and lead us not into temptation, but deliver us from evil. For Thine, is the Kingdom, and the Power, and the Glory now and forever. Amen.

~

This poem describes the first Church.

My Church

My church has but one temple
Wide as the world is wide
Set with a million stars
Where millions of hearts abide.

My church has no creed to bar
A simple brother man
But says, "Come thou and worship"
To everyone who can.

My church has no roof or walls,
Nor floors save the beautiful sod –
For fear, I will seem to limit
The love of the illimitable God.

From: Best Loved Poems of the American People Copyright 1936;
Doubleday and Company – Wikipedia

The Christophers motto:

"It is better to light one candle, than to curse the darkness."

~

Dawning

Love coming like the dawn;
Sensing, not perceived,
Silently, softly, slowly,

Surely, clearly, firmly,
Enfolding, completely,
Love coming like the dawn. PA. B. (1978)

~

Let us continue to change current events here at home and abroad; we can all pray. Start with a simple thank you to Spirit for each new day. Say thank you to all who give assistance, even in the smallest way. Thank the Creator of the Universe. Encourage family and friends to do the same.

~

One of the basic tenets of our Constitution guarantees freedom of religion, and our national motto is:

In God We Trust

Let us get back to the faith of our founding fathers.

God hears our prayers. When you call someone on the telephone, you know who it is you are talking to, even though you cannot see them. God hears us in the same way. Talk with God the way you do with your closest friend. You will get answers through *inspiration—in-spir(it)-ion. (Dr. Wayne Dyer)*

~

We all have favorite songs and poems that inspire us. Reading from these favorites can make a big difference in our daily routines. Don't be afraid to sing them out loud. Father Bowling, the pastor of one of the parishes I attended, insisted that the whole congregation *must sing.* Father couldn't carry a tune in a bucket. He told us that to sing was to praise twice. You could hear him throughout the 1,500 seat church. Everybody sang.

~

POETRY: This poem, written by Rudyard Kipling in 1909, after the Boer War, 1895 in Africa, sets a bar that we can all live by. For a very interesting history of this poem, go to the website: www.dailymail.co.uk/news.

IF

If you can keep your head when all about you
Are losing theirs and blaming it on you;
If you can trust yourself when all men doubt you,

But make allowance for their doubting too.
If you can wait and not be tired by waiting,
Or being lied about, don't deal in lies,
Or being hated, don't deal in hate,
And don't look too good, nor talk too wise:

If you can dream, and not make dreams your master;
If you can think, and not make thoughts your aim;
If you can meet with Triumph and Disaster
And treat these two imposters just the same;
If you can bear to hear the truth you've spoken
Twisted by knaves to make a trap for fools,
Or watch the things you gave your life to, broken,
And stoop and build 'em up with worn out tools:

If you can make one heap of all your winnings
And risk it on one turn of pitch-and-toss,
And lose, and start again at your beginnings
And never breathe a word about your loss;
If you can force you heart and nerve and sinew
To serve your turn long after they are gone,
And so hold on when there is nothing in you
Except the Will which says to them "Hold On!"

If you can talk with crowds and keep your virtue,
Or walk with kings – nor lose the common touch,
If neither friend or foe can hurt you,
If all men count with you, but none too much;
If you can fill the unforgiving minute
With sixty seconds' worth of distance run,
Yours is the earth and everything that is in it,
And – which is more – you'll be a man my son.

~

A beautiful song by Cat Stevens "Morning has Broken" is a beautiful way to greet the new day. The original is said to have been written by St. Patrick with the title being: "Morning Has Broken." The words to this version are beautiful too.

The following is a song that is from the OCP book of the Masses and songs for the whole year. It struck a chord for me; I hope that it does for you too. It is a call to take that step in Faith.

THE SUMMONS

Will you come and follow me, If I but call your name?
Will you go where you don't know, And never be the same?
Will you let my love be shown, Will you let my name be known?
Will you let my life be grown in you, And you in me"

Will you leave yourself behind, If I but call your name?
Will you care for cruel or kind, And never be the same?
Will you risk the hostile stare, Should your life attract or scare?
Will you let me answer prayer in you, And you in me?

Will you let the blinded see, If I but call your name?
Will you set the prisoner free, And never be the same?
Will you kiss the leper clean, And do such as this unseen?
And admit to what I mean in you, And you in me?

Will you love the "you" you hide, If I but call your name?
Will you quell the fear inside, And never be the same?
Will you use the faith you've found, To shape the world around?
Through my sight and touch and sound in you, And you in me?

Lord your summons echoes true, When you but call my name.
Let me turn and follow you, And never be the same.
In your company I'll go, Where your love and your footsteps show.
Thus I'll move and live and grow in you, And you in me.

By God's grace, no matter how small or weak our one voice, added to other voices joined in the same cause—protecting ourselves and our freedoms as given to us through our Constitution, united we will be heard around the world.

~

"There is a tide in the affairs of men, which taken at the flood, leads on to fortune. Omitted, all the voyage of their life is bound in shallows and in miseries. On such a full sea are we now afloat. And we must take the current when it serves, or lose our ventures." **Julius Caesar Act 4, Scene 3.**

Thank you and we'll make our voices heard, all through this next twelve months, on Face Book, on Twitter, by e-mail and most important the Voting Booth in November 2014. **God Bless you and God Bless America.** - - Patricia Ann Burns

~

NOTE: September 18, 2014, was the 51st Anniversary of the March on Washington commemorated today.

The Price of Freedom is Vigilance and Participation

Democracy is the ultimate test in governance. Ours is the longest lasting Democracy in history to date. Because all who vote for the people in office, it is up to us to make sure they are doing their job and we are the only nation in the world that have this type of government.

In order to preserve what we have and continue to meet the diverse need of all nationalities (people from every country in the world) we have to put all differences and past injuries aside. *We are all Americans now, standing together, working for the good of our whole people. And a special welcome to all new to our shores.*

THE VALUE OF PATRIOTISM
IS INVALUABLE

America The Beautiful
Land Of The Free and
The Home Of The Brave

PATRIOTISM

1941 - The majority of Americans born today do not remember the blackouts during World War II.

Not a light, from border to border or coast to coast, could be seen after sundown. Many secret areas in the country were camouflaged even in the daytime. Signs were posted all over the country with a picture of Uncle Sam (an older gent, had a top hat with the stars and stripes around it. His faced showed the wrinkles that come with age, he had a white goatee.)

His clothes were patriotic too. He held a finger to his lips—a message to mean, d*on't let anything slip from your month, you didn't know who would be listening*. There was an assortment of signs like this one. Another one was of Uncle Sam turned straight forward, right arm stretching straight out forward, from his shoulder with his finger pointing, with the caption reading: "Uncle Sam Needs You Now." These posters were very colorful in red, white and blue.

It was also the time of the USO – United Service Organization, run by volunteers, who provided a place for all service personal to have a retreat when they were so far from home. Hollywood's talented stars were some of the first to step up and volunteer their spare time, to entertain those in service. They were at the forefront of conducting war bond drives to raise money to support the war. (Go to the WWII War Bonds site.)

Bob Hope was on the go all over the world, all through the war with his Hollywood volunteers and put on shows. I hope to see the day again when we have this fervor of patriotism and love of our country. There were the troop trains, carrying service men and women back and forth, across the country; these were *express trains*, regular service trains were side-lined for these trains to get through. Again, go the web and to your libraries, it was quite a time here, very serious and very hopeful. Besides, the Army, Navy, Marines and the U. S. Army Air Corps, there also were the Seabees, and of course, the WACS-Army, WAVES-Navy, and women Marines, who filled office administrative support positions. There was also a branch of women airplane pilots ferrying to the destination where they were needed during the war. PBS showed a program about these women in service, known as WASPS-Women Air Force Service Pilots.

The majority of immigrants came to our shores to escape unacceptable conditions in their former homeland. They have had firsthand experience in dealing with the unbearable strife and threat to their lives in many far too many cases; the influx now is from all over globe.

For more than 200 years, the American flag has been the symbol of our nation's strength and unity. It's been a source of pride and inspiration for millions of citizens. And the American Flag has been a prominent icon in our national history. Here are the highlights of its unique past.

On January 1, 1776, the Continental Army was reorganized in accordance with a Congressional resolution which placed American forces under General George Washington's control. On New Year's Day, the Continental Army was laying siege to Boston which had been taken over by the British Army. Washington ordered the Grand Union flag hoisted above his base at Prospect Hill. It had 13 alternate red and white stripes and the British Union Jack in the upper left-hand corner (the canton.)

In May of 1976, Betsy Ross reported that she sewed the first American flag.

On June 24, 1777, in order to establish an official flag for the new nation, the Continental Congress passed the first Flag Act; "Resolved: The flag of the United States be made of thirteen stripes, alternate red and white; that the union be thirteen stars, white in a blue field, representing a new constellation."

Between 1777 and 1960 Congress passed several acts that changed the design and arrangement of the flag and allowed for additional stars and stripes to be added to reflect the admission of each new state.

- Act of January 13, 1794 – provided for 15 stripes and 15 stars after May 1795.
- Act of April 4, 1818 – provided for 13 stripes and one star for each state, to be added to the flag on the 4th of July, following the admission of each new state, signed by President Monroe.
- Executive order of President Taft dated June 24, 1912 – established proportions of the flag and provided for arrangement of the stars in six rows horizontally and vertically.
- Executive Order of President Eisenhower dated January 3, 1959 – provided for the arrangement of the stars in seven rows of seven stars each, staggered horizontally and vertically.
- Executive Order of President Eisenhower dated August 21, 1959 – provided for the arrangement of the stars in nine rows staggered horizontally and eleven rows of stars staggered vertically.

Today the flag consists of thirteen horizontal stripes, seven red alternating with 6 white. The stripes represent the original 13 colonies the stars represent the 50 states of the Union. The colors of the flag are symbolic as well: Red symbolizes Hardiness and Valor, White symbolizes Purity and Blue represents Vigilance, Perseverance and Justice.

The history of the Pledge of Allegiance is two pages long so I am just excerpting key points; go to the website www.ushistory.org/documents/pledge.

The Pledge of Allegiance was written in August 1892 by the socialist minister Francis Bellamy (1855-1931). It was originally published in *The Youth's Companion* on September 8, 1892.

Bellamy had hoped that the pledge would be used by citizens in any country

In its original form it read:

"I pledge allegiance to my Flag and the Republic, for which it stands, one nation, indivisible, with liberty and justice for all."

Further history, and then in 1954, in response to the Communist threat of the times, President Eisenhower encouraged Congress to add the words "under God," creating the 31-word pledge we recite today. Bellamy's daughter objected to this alteration. Over her objections, today it reads as the President encouraged.

THE PLEDGE OF ALLEGIANCE

I pledge allegiance to the flag,
Of the United States of America,
And to the republic for which it stands,
One nation under God, indivisible
With Liberty and Justice, for all.

The article continues with the proper form and stance for reciting the Pledge of the military and lay people. Military personnel give a formal salute and all lay people, including children, should put his/her right hand over the heart, standing at attention, while the pledge is being said or passing by.

Holidays to display your Flag

New Year's Day	Inauguration Day
Martin Luther King Day	Lincoln's Birthday
Washington's Birthday	Easter Sunday
Patriots Day, April 19	
National Day of Prayer, First Thursday in May	
Mother's Day	Armed Forces Day
Memorial Day **half-day until noon) then at full mast**	
Flag Day	Independence Day, July 4th

Labor Day
Columbus Day, October 12th
Veterans Day
Christmas Day

Constitution Day
Navy Day
Thanksgiving Day
Election Days

and such other days as may be proclaimed by the President of the United States.

Flying the American Flag at Half Staff
When should the flag be flown
at half-staff?

In the early days of our country, no regulations existed for flying the flag at half-staff and as result there were many conflicting policies. But on March 1, 1954, President Dwight Eisenhower issued a proclamation on the proper times.

- The flag should fly at half-staff for 30 days at all federal buildings grounds and naval vessels throughout the United States and it territories and possessions after the:
- Death of the President

It is to fly 10 days at half-staff after the death of the
- The vice president,
- The chief justice of the United States Supreme Court
- The retired chief justice of the United States Supreme Court
- The speaker of the House of Representatives

From the day of death until interment
- A former vice president
- An associated justice of the Supreme Court
- A member of the Cabinet
- The president pro tempore of the Senate
- The majority leader of the Senate
- The minority leader of the Senate
- The majority leader of the House of Representatives

- The minority leader of the House of Representatives

On the day and the day after death of a senator, representative territorial delegate or the:
- Resident-commissioner from the Commonwealth of Puerto Rico

Upon the death of the governor of a state, territory or possession, the flag should be flown at half-staff on all facilities in that governor's state, congressional district, territory or commonwealth of these officials.

- When the whole nations is in mourning.
- On Memorial Day the flag should be flown at half-staff from sunrise until noon only, then raised briskly to the top of the staff until sunset, in honor of the nation's battle heroes.*

*On all days that the flag is flown at half-mast: 'The flag should be briskly run up to the top of the staff before being lowered *slowly* to the half-staff position.

State and Local Holidays

Your State Birthday – see www.usflag.org/flagholidays.html
~

The late Ray Charles worked to have *AMERICA THE BEAUTIFUL* become our NATIONAL ANTHEM. As the words in this song show, they have a strong, vigorous, challenging and inspiring history. The time has come for: *AMERICA THE BEAUTIFUL* to become our *NATIONAL ANTHEM.*

In my view, America the Beautiful tells the story of who we are and our history of struggle to defend and protect our Bill of Rights and where we are striving to go. Life is meant to be a struggle; it is the way that human nature truly learns of what is most valuable. Through our struggles we will eventually be successful if we develop the staying power through perseverance to always strive for the common good

Since I was a child, I have always loved a parade. And I love anything connected with patriotism. John Phillips Sousa* is another of my all-time favorites. Since I have looked up the history of the Flag and the Pledge of Allegiance, I thought, I couldn't let the history of the song, America the Beautiful, be left out. I am so happy that I have. It is the best argument to give the view of Ray Charles and so many who truly love this song to give it second consideration.

www.marineband.usmc.mil/...john-sousa
*John Phillip Sousa 1854 – 1932: Was the leader of "The President's Own" United States Marine Band for 12 years. Under his guidance, he brought the band "To an unprecedented level of excellence: a standard upheld by every Marine Band Director since."

In 1888 he wrote "Semper Fidelis" (Always Faithful) "Dedicated to the officers and men of the Marine Corps." and is known as the "official" March of the Marine Corps."

All due respects to the Star Spangled Banner, it celebrates specifically one event, although the ideal has certainly carried throughout our history. I would like America to be celebrated for all of the beauty and good, and the accomplishments starting with pilgrims feet, crossing the plains to open up the west, as written in the song America the Beautiful. Please do go to this website; it has a picture of Katherine Lee Bates in her younger years and a picture of her later in life.

NOTE: Because of copyright laws, the full words of a song may not be published in full without consent. Copy Right laws are in effect for 70 years, then expire.

www.pikespeak.com, America's Mountain website posted:

The song that was "almost" National Anthem of the United States of America was America the Beautiful.

In 1893, Katherine Lee Bates, an English teacher at Wellesley College in Massachusetts, agreed to take a summer teaching position at Colorado College in Colorado Springs, CO. During her 2,000 mile train trip through Chicago, Kansas and into Colorado, the 34-year-old Bates became quite impressed with the beauty and vastness of the United States.

One of the perks of being a visiting professor was a carriage ride up Pike's Peak. The horse-drawn carriage could go no further than the Halfway House (Glen Cove), so they switched to burros for the remaining six miles of the trip.

After reveling in the views after only a half hour on the summit of Pike's Peak, they descended again. On the way down, she wrote in her diary:

"...we stood at last on the Gate-of-Heaven summit...and gazed in wordless rapture over the far expanse of mountain ranges and the sea-like sweep of plain."

After she returned to her room in the Antler's Hotel that night, she remarked to friends that countries such as England had failed because, while they may have been "great" they had not been "good" and that "unless we are willing to crown our greatness with goodness, and our bounty with brotherhood, our beloved America may go the same way."

Because of her experiences on that trip, she later wrote a poem, which has now become our classic anthem "America the Beautiful.

The original four stanzas were printed on July 4, 1895 in an issue of the Congregationalist newspaper. After several revisions, the final poem was published at the *Boston Evening Transcript* nine years later.

Samual Ward's hymn, "Meterna" was selected as the music behind the lyrics. However, Ward died in 1903 and never knew how popular Bates' lyrics and his music would become.

A strong push was made to adopt the hymn as the national anthem in 1926. However, President Hoover chose the "Star-Spangled Banner" instead.

In 1993, 100 years after Bates ascended Pike's Peak, Colorado Springs' businessman, Costas Rombocos donated an "America the Beautiful" monument that was placed atop Pikes Peak. The monument can be seen on the observation platform to the south of the Summit House.

While Bates retained the copyright on her poem to protect it, she never sought any payment of royalties. It was her personal gift to the country.

AMERICA THE BEAUTIFUL

O beautiful for spacious skies, For amber waves of grain,
For purple mountains majesty, Above the fruited plain,
America! America! God shed His grace on thee,
And crown thy good, with brotherhood,
From sea to shining sea.

O beautiful for pilgrim feet, Whose stern impassioned stress,
A thoroughfare for freedom beat, Across the wilderness,
America! America! God mend, Thine ev'ry flaw,
Confirm thy soul in self-control, Thy liberty in law.

I want to add a stanza that I have written for our military today.

O beautiful, who through the years
Our veterans did defend,
Our lands, our seas, our skies above
By those who heard the call,
Brave defenders, men and women too
Gave life and limb for all,
Their glories writ large on life's page
A legacy for all.

O beautiful for heroes proved, In liberating strife
Who more than self, their country loved,
And mercy more than life,
America! America! May God thy gold refine,
Till all success be nobleness, And every gain Divine.

O beautiful for patriot dream, that sees beyond the years,
Thine alabaster cities gleam, Undimmed by human tears!
America! America! God shed His grace on thee,
And crown thy good in brotherhood,
From sea to shining sea.

It is my hope to continue to call for this change. Take time to really read the words and think about our history. Especially today when a change in direction is needed to continue to work that was set in our Constitution and Bill of Rights—LIBERTY AND JUSTICE FOR ALL.

Continue to peruse the web and look up the history of these songs and the important documents that enshrine the ideals; the basis for who we are as a people and a country as a whole. Read them slowly and carefully, they are uplifting.

"My Country 'Tis of Thee" is the National Hymn of the United States. I always thought the title was "America." When looking for it on the web, the response was for "America the Beautiful" as noted above. "My Country 'tis of Thee," was written by Samuel F. Smith (of the Baptist faith,) a student at Andover Theological Seminary in Andover, MA. It is also known as AMERICA.

"My Country 'Tis Of Thee: was written to fulfill a drive of Samuel Smith to create a national hymn for the United States. In about 30 minutes on a rainy day, he wrote the now classic anthem. The first three verses encourage and invoke national pride, while the last verse was specifically reserved as a petition to God for His continued favor and protection of the United States of America. It was first performed on July 4, 1832 at the Park Street Church in

178

Boston, MA. Further history can be found at **www.allabouthistory.org** /my-country-tis-of-thee.

MY COUNTRY 'TIS OF THEE

My country 'tis of thee,
Sweet land of liberty,
Of thee I sing;
Land where my fathers died;
Land of the pilgrims' pride,
From every mountainside,
Let freedom ring!

My native country thee,
Land of the noble free,
Thy name I love;
I love the rock and rills,
Thy woods and tempered hills;
My heart with rapture thrills,
Like that above.

Let music swell the breeze,
And ring from all the trees,
Sweet freedom's song;
Let mortals tongues awake
Let all that breathe partake;
Let rocks their silence break;
The sound prolong.

Our fathers' God to thee,
Author of liberty,
To Thee we sing;
Long may our land be bright,
With freedom's holy light,
Protect us by Thy might,
Great God our King.

Again, the history of this song is fascinating; *please go* to the website to read the complete story. The song was written by Francis Scott Key…35 year old lawyer…who observed the action from the boat he was on…"It seemed as though mother earth had opened and was vomiting shot and shell in a sheet of fire and brimstone," Key wrote later. But when darkness arrived, Key saw only red erupting in the night sky. Given the scale of the attack, he was certain the British would win. The hours passed slowly, but in the clearing smoke of "the dawn's early light" on September 14, he saw the American Flag—not the British Union Jack—flying over the fort, announcing an American victory. www.smithsonianmag.com

THE STAR SPANGLED BANNER

O say can you see,
By the dawn's early light;
What so proudly we hail,
At the twilight's last gleaming,
Whose broad stripes and bright stars,
through the perilous night,
O're the ramparts we watch,
were so gallantly gleaming;
And the rockets red glare,
the bombs bursting mid-air,

Gave proof through the night,
that our flag was still there.
O say does that Star Spangled Banner yet wave,
O're the land of the free,
and the home of the brave.

The following song was composed in 1940. The lyrics – Don Raye and music – Al Jacobs   Wikipedia.org.

This song was written in 1940 by the above team. They were a talented duo having worked in vaudeville and turned to song writing. They collaborated with many of Hollywood's notable composers and musicians and wrote many songs that were very popular. Another song of theirs that was very popular during World War II "Boogie Woogie Bugle Boy" which won a nomination for an Oscar in 1941. This is a song that will get you on your feet dancing.

This song starts: "...a famous trumpet man... He had a boogie style...He's in the army now, a-blowin reveille; He's the boogie—woogie bugle boy from company B..." I can hear the Andrew Sisters singing it now, Patty, Maxine and La Vern.

THIS IS MY COUNTRY

This is my country... then the end

I pledge thee my allegiance
America the Bold
For this is my country
To have and to hold.

This next song was written by George M. Cohan, 1906 (wikipedia.org), and first performed on February 6, 1906 on opening night at Herald Square Theater in New York City...quickly became the first song from a musical to sell over a million copies of sheet music. Cohan got the idea from a Civil War veteran who fought at Gettysburg...holding a carefully folded but ragged old flag. The man reportedly turned and said "She's a grand old rag...the public did not like the flag being called a rag as in the original song, so Cohan changed the title to She's A Grand Old Flag. Mostly known today for the chorus; it has four verses, but the chorus is what is usually sung.

YOU'RE A GRAND OLD FLAG
Chorus:

You're a grand old flag,
You're a high flying flag
And forever in peace may you wave.

You're the emblem of,
The land I love,
The home of the free and the brave.

Ev'ry heart beats true
'neath the Red, White and Blue,
There, there's never a boast or brag.
But should auld acquaintance be forgot,
Keep your eye on the grand old flag.

Julia Ward wrote the words to:

THE BATTLE HYMN OF THE REPUBLIC in 1861 using the music from the song "John Brown's Body". It was first published in the *Atlantic Monthly in February 1862* Wikipedia.org

THE BATTLE HYMN OF THE REPUBLIC

CHORUS – There are six verses to this song.

Glory, glory, hallelujah!
Glory, glory, hallelujah!
Glory, glory, hallelujah!
His truth is marching on.

Mine eyes have seen the glory of the coming of the Lord;
He is trampling out the vintage where the grapes of wrath are stored;
He hath loosed the fateful lightning of His terrible swift sword.
His truth is marching on.

CHORUS

I have seen Him in the watch-fires of a hundred circling camps,
They have builded Him an altar of evening dews and damps;
I can read His righteous sentence by the dim and flaring lamps;
His day is marching on.
CHORUS

I have read a fiery gospel writ in burnished rows of steel:
'As ye deal with my contemners so with you my grace shall deal;
Let the Hero, born of woman crush the serpent with his heel,
Since God is marching on.

CHORUS

The song: THE BATLE CRY OF FREEDOM was written in 1862 by George Frederick Root during the Civil War and was Lincoln's Presidential Campaign song. Wikipedia.org.

BATTLE CRY OF FREEDOM...

CHORUS
The Union forever! Hurrah, boys hurrah!
Down with the traitors, up with the stars;
While we rally round the flag, boys, rally once again,
Shouting the battle cry of freedom.
VERSE
Yes we'll rally round the flag, boys, we'll rally once again,
shouting the battle cry of freedom,
We will rally from the hillside, we'll gather from the plain,
Shouting the battle cry of freedom.

CHORUS

VERSE
W springing to the call of our brothers gone before,
Shouting the battle cry of freedom!
And we'll fill our vacant ranks with a million freemen more.
Shouting the battle cry of freedom.

CHORUS

VERSE
We will welcome to our numbers the loyal, true and brave,
Shouting the battle cry of freedom!

183

And although they may be poor, not a man shall be a slave,
Shouting the battle cry of Freedom.

CHORUS

VERSE
So we're spring to the call from the East and from the West,
Shouting the battle of Freedom;
And we'll hurl rebel crew from the land that we love best,
Shouting the battle cry of Freedom.

CHORUS

SOME OTHER FAVORITES

From a list of 100 songs, including Rock, Country and Classic (list compiled by Aly Adair, Yahoo Contributor), following are the top eight:

1. God Bless America – sung by Kate Smith
2. Living in the Promised Land – Willie Nelson
3. Travelin' Soldier – The Dixie Chicks
4. I'm Proud To Be an American – Lee Greenwood
5. This Land Is Your Land – Woodie Guthrie
6. Born in the USA – Bruce Springsteen

7. More Than A Name On The Wall – Statler Brothers
8. Some Gave All – Billy Ray Cyrus

And finally I think that although this is not a Patriotic Song per se, we can include it in the list of favorites, because it is fair to say that the people that make up who we are, here in America, have our origins and are from countries around the globe.

~

WE ARE THE LIGHT OF THE WORLD AND OUR LIGHT SHINES BEFORE ALL MEN

Written by Michael Jackson and Lionel Ritchie

WE ARE THE WORLD

CHORUS

We are the world, We are the children,
We are the ones who make a brighter day,
So let's start giving, There's a choice were making…

And as we move forward, God Bless America!

~

CONCLUSION

In opening the book with the words of President John F. Kennedy, I will close with an excerpt (taken from James David Barber's book The Presidential Character) and from his notebook 1945-46; he wrote:

"To be a positive force for the public good in politics one must have three things; a solid moral code governing his public actions, a broad knowledge of our institutions and traditions and a specific background in the technical problems of our institutions and traditions, and a specific background in the technical problems of government, and lastly he must have political appeal—the gift of winning public confidence and support."

John F. Kennedy

~

This is a simple message and a hard one to put into practice.
Be can always try through the voting booth. It is our duty to freedom, here and everywhere in the world.

P. A. B.
September 21, 2014

ADDED THOUGHTS

The book **THE GREAT THOUGHTS** is a compilation of some outstanding observations of world history as described on the cover of the book: "From Abelard to Zola, from Ancient Greece to contemporary America, the ideas that have shaped the history of the world." The work is from the pen of George Seldes, *Muckraker,* Journalist/Press Critic, Author; 1890-995.

The term muckraker was used in the early 20th century. After World War II 'whistle blower' came into use. Both of these words have always had a bad connotation—as if someone is wrong for shining a light on wrong doing. It is time now to pay attention to these warnings and not put the person(s) down. Paul Revere was credited for saving our country with his cry "the British are coming".

Concerned Citizen(s) are raising their voices everywhere; here at home and around the world. I am a Concerned Citizen and the messenger for all of the voices that have been raise through the internet.

I have become an ardent fan the late George Seldes. Dissatisfied with the way events were unfolding, he accepted the label "muckraker" and in the process accepted the ridicule too. He continued throughout his career to call attention to wrong doing where ever his travels took him as a reporter.

I read his Introduction to this book and I have joined a new generation of people who seek to know the truth: John 8:32 - For you shall know the truth and the truth shall make you free. The quotes in his book **GREAT THOUGHTS** are not 'good' thoughts, but words from both good and evil people throughout history.

I would like to make this suggestion: If you are dissatisfied with the way our government stands at this moment become, a 'muckraker'. This word is no longer in use. However 'Concerned Citizen' is most appropriate. We need people who will stand up

187

and say 'enough of corruption and disloyalty.' and speak up for truth. Call out all people painting our Constitution black with shame, throughout our Government, our Courts, Businesses, Entertainment and home life, destroying our most precious values now spreading like a wildfire throughout our country with corruption.

What greater way to serve those 1,500,000,00 returning veterans, now live among, us that are maimed, have PTSD, or both? What better way to serve those who fought and died to protect these Freedoms For Us?

What greater way to say enough to those anarchists that are trying tear down the Door To Freedom?

What greater way than to follow all of those maligned 'Whistle Blowers' who dared to stand up for Truth and Justice throughout our history. (And a Special Thank You to all, who are hanging in the fray even though you can still barely be heard above the systems being jammed—help is on the way.)

NOW is the time to answer President John F. Kennedy's call for All Americans to "Ask not what your country can do for you. Ask what You Can Do For Your Country."

All past attempts for Democracy, to be continue as a viable and strong government, have failed because no one would speak up to show where and how the Ship of State is going way off course. Because we have an open government for the good of the people, it is also the most lucrative for those, who for personal gain, will go to any length to tear our system down. Use this book as a sure guide to keep you on target. I am sure Mr. Seldes, after his 25 years of compiling this information, finished at age 95 would feel well rewarded.

Qualifications to act in this capacity include: To know and tell the truth without reservation; loyalty only to God and your 'self'; and a very strong constitution to stand by your convictions at all costs. Thanks to all, who are already on this path to Freedom.

**Concerned Citizens are the Heralds of
Truth and the Guardians of Freedom**

JOIN NOW

"You can only protect your liberties in this world by protecting the other man's freedom. You can only be free if I am free."

Clarence Darrow, American Lawyer

Addressed to jury, Communist trial, Chicago, 1920

Protect Your Rights,   Protect My Rights,   Protect All Rights,

BECOME GUARNTORS FOR ALL AMERICANS.

STAND UP! STAND UP   STAND UP FOR AMERICA

STAND UP NOW!